Boyhood

Boyhood appeared in 2014, having followed the same cast of characters for more than a decade while focusing on young Mason, whose educational, personal, and family life were cast upon the screen in poignant and often painful detail. Renowned director Richard Linklater chronicled Mason's story from first grade to high school graduation as the boy ventured toward manhood, enduring his parents' divorce, his mother's troubled remarriages, his tenuous relationship with his father, and his evolving struggles to understand his own growing pains. Meanwhile, the United States was recovering from 9/11, enduring two wars and the Great Recession, electing an African American president, and adjusting to life constantly connected to the internet. The unprecedented production resulted in a film that went on to become one of the most honored stories of youth in Hollywood history.

Timothy Shary traces the development of *Boyhood* from its audacious concept through its tenacious production to its celebrated reception, placing it within the context of cinematic parables about children to demonstrate its distinctive vision. The author of numerous studies on the history of teen cinema, Shary evaluates the film's many messages about youth and adolescence within the context of early twenty-first century American culture, illuminating how Linklater's singular vision of the otherwise ordinary life of a boy reveals potent universal truths about all people.

Timothy Shary has published seven books on the representational politics of age and gender, beginning with *Generation Multiplex: The Image of Youth in Contemporary American Cinema* (2002, 2014) and most recently *Fade to Gray: Aging in American Cinema* (2016) with Nancy McVittie. His work on youth cinema has been published in numerous books and journals since the 1990s, including *The Journal of Film and Video, Film Quarterly, The Journal of Popular Culture, The Journal of Popular Film and Television,* and *Boyhood Studies.*

Cinema and Youth Cultures
Series Editors: Siân Lincoln & Yannis Tzioumakis

Cinema and Youth Cultures engages with well-known youth films from American cinema as well the cinemas of other countries. Using a variety of methodological and critical approaches the series volumes provide informed accounts of how young people have been represented in film, while also exploring the ways in which young people engage with films made for and about them. In doing this, the Cinema and Youth Cultures series contributes to important and long-standing debates about youth cultures, how they are mobilized and articulated in influential film texts, and the impact that these texts have had on popular culture at large.

Clueless
Lesley Speed

Boyhood
Timothy Shary

Grease
Barbara Jane Brickman

www.routledge.com/Cinema-and-Youth-Cultures/book-series/CYC

Boyhood
A Young Life on Screen

Timothy Shary

Figure FM.1 Boyhood, 2014: Ellar Coltrane. Director: Richard Linklater. Card/poster.

Image courtesy of Filmproducer/RES/Shutterstock

Routledge
Taylor & Francis Group

LONDON AND NEW YORK

First published 2018 by Routledge

2 Park Square, Milton Park, Abingdon, Oxon, OX14 4RN
605 Third Avenue, New York, NY 10017

Routledge is an imprint of the Taylor & Francis Group, an informa business

First issued in paperback 2020

British Library Cataloguing-in-Publication Data
A catalogue record for this book is available from the British Library

Library of Congress Cataloging-in-Publication Data
Names: Shary, Timothy, 1967– author.
Title: Boyhood : a young life on screen / Timothy Shary.
Description: London ; New York : Routledge, 2018. | Series: Cinema
    and youth cultures | Includes bibliographical references and index.
Identifiers: LCCN 2017034768 | ISBN 9781138682443 (hardback : alk.
    paper) | ISBN 9781315545103 (ebook)
Subjects: LCSH: Boyhood (Motion picture) | Coming-of-age films—
    History and criticism.
Classification: LCC PN1997.2.B69 S53 2018 | DDC 791.43/72—dc23
LC record available at https://lccn.loc.gov/2017034768

ISBN: 978-1-138-68244-3 (hbk)
ISBN: 978-0-367-73563-0 (pbk)

Typeset in Times New Roman
by Apex CoVantage, LLC

**To Olivia Xendolyn
and her wonderful girlhood**

Contents

Figures

Series editors' introduction

Despite the high visibility of youth films in the global media marketplace, especially since the 1980s when Conglomerate Hollywood realized that such films were not only strong box office performers but also the starting point for ancillary sales in other media markets as well as for franchise building, academic studies that focused specifically on such films were slow to materialize. Arguably the most important factor behind academia's reluctance to engage with youth films was a (then) widespread perception within the Film and Media Studies communities that such films held little cultural value and significance, and therefore were not worthy of serious scholarly research and examination. Just like the young subjects they represented, whose interests and cultural practices have been routinely deemed transitional and transitory, so were the films that represented them perceived as fleeting and easily digestible, destined to be forgotten quickly, as soon as the next youth film arrived on cinema screens a week later.

Under these circumstances, and despite a small number of pioneering studies in the 1980s and early 1990s, the field of 'youth film studies' did not really start blossoming and attracting significant scholarly attention until the 2000s and in combination with similar developments in cognate areas such as 'girl studies.' However, because of the paucity of material in the previous decades, the majority of these new studies in the 2000s focused primarily on charting the field and therefore steered clear of long, in-depth examinations of youth films or were exemplified by edited collections that chose particular films to highlight certain issues to the detriment of others. In other words, despite providing often wonderfully rich accounts of youth cultures as they have been captured by key films, these studies could not have possibly dedicated sufficient space to engage with more than just a few key aspects of youth films.

In more recent (post-2010) years a number of academic studies started delimiting their focus and therefore providing more space for in-depth examinations of key types of youth films, such as slasher films, biker films, or youth films in particular historical periods. From that point on, it was a matter of time for the first publications that focused exclusively on key youth films from a number of perspectives to appear (*Mamma Mia! The Movie*, *Twilight* and *Dirty Dancing* are among the first films to receive this treatment). Conceived primarily as edited collections, these studies provided a multifaceted analysis of these films, focusing on such issues as the politics of representing youth, the stylistic and narrative choices that characterize these films and the extent to which they are representative of a youth cinema, the ways these films address their audiences, the ways youth audiences engage with these films, the films' industrial location, and other relevant issues.

It is within this increasingly maturing and expanding academic environment that the **Cinema and Youth Cultures** volumes arrive, aiming to consolidate existing knowledge, provide new perspectives, apply innovative methodological approaches, offer sustained and in-depth analyses of key films and therefore become the 'go to' resource for students and scholars interested in theoretically informed, authoritative accounts of youth cultures in film. As editors, we have tried to be as inclusive as possible in our selection of key examples of youth films by commissioning volumes on films that span the history of cinema, including the silent film era; that portray contemporary youth cultures as well as ones associated with particular historical periods; that represent examples of mainstream and independent cinema; that originate in American cinema and the cinemas of other nations; and that attracted significant critical attention and commercial success during their initial release or were 'rediscovered' after an unpromising initial critical reception. Together these volumes are going to advance youth film studies while also being able to offer extremely detailed examinations of films that are now considered significant contributions to cinema and our cultural life more broadly.

We hope readers will enjoy the series.

Siân Lincoln and Yannis Tzioumakis
Cinema and Youth Cultures Series Editors

Acknowledgments

My first thanks go to Yannis Tzioumakis and Siân Lincoln, for inviting me to be part of this series and for directing me through the process of writing about this compelling and often challenging film.

Since I began working on this project in late 2014, many friends (from the field and beyond) have shared ideas and provoked debates that often found their way into my comments here: Chris Boucher, Christopher Goodwin, Daniel Smith-Rowsey, Dave Johnson, Diane Ogden, Emily Hansen, Jon Lupo, Louisa Stein, Mary Harrod, Mike Boucher, Mike Rennett, Patrick O'Neill, Pete Kunze, and Richard Brown. My thanks to all of you, and to anyone I may have omitted.

I further thank my colleagues in the Cinema and Youth Cultures series with whom I have been able to share work and sympathies as we've embarked on this exciting endeavor: Andy Scahill, Barbara Jane Brickman, Catherine Driscoll, Elissa Nelson, Lesley Speed, and Tim McNelis.

And a particular thanks to Richard Linklater, of course – not only for creating the subject of this analysis, but for answering some questions and giving me a more complete understanding of *Boyhood*.

Introduction

If cinema was a painting, time would be the paint itself.

– Richard Linklater[1]

Time is an inescapable force in our lives, and its impact has had an unmistakable presence in the films of Richard Linklater since his debut feature *Slacker* (1991), which became a sensation on the revivified indie film scene when he was 30. Before this breakout hit, the young man had made some inroads to learning filmmaking through short and experimental efforts during the later 1980s, and with his first longer film, the unreleased *It's Impossible to Learn to Plow by Reading Books* (1988), he already indicated his curiosities about the passage of time and the mercurial nature of life's events. The genius of *Slacker* was at least as much in its form as its content, a loosely connected narrative of stories told by relatively random (primarily young) denizens of Austin, Texas, who seem to have little direction in life and little worry about lacking it. The story, such as it is, unfolds over a day and night in the lives of disparate people with no clear histories and scant sense of evolution in their actions.

Timing was also a contributing factor in the success of *Slacker*, because it arrived just months after the publication of Douglas Coupland's influential novel *Generation X: Tales for an Accelerated Culture* (1991), which traced the stories of disaffected young people in southern California struggling to find an identity different from the Baby Boomer generation that had preceded them. (See Figure 0.1.) Linklater had originally associated the term 'slacker' with 'avoiding duties and responsibilities' and knew of its WWI usage for draft dodgers, so he applied it within the film to these characters who appeared to be embracing 'individual freedom and thinking in a new way' (Klosterman 2005, p. 72). Even though he did not intend to make a polemic about popular culture, an association quickly formed in the collective conscience that viewed the postponed adults of Generation X as 'slackers.'

Figure 0.1 In his debut release *Slacker,* Richard Linklater played one of the many
wandering characters, here contemplating reality and dreams in the back
of a cab

Linklater would go on to consider concerns of youth and time in subsequent features, including his next three films, *Dazed and Confused* (1993),
Before Sunrise (1995), and *SubUrbia* (1996). He remained committed to
relatively low-budget independent productions but soon began expanding
his range of narrative topics with the historical gangster story *The Newton
Boys* (1998), the animated meditation *Waking Life* (2001), and his biggest
commercial success, the Jack Black comedy *School of Rock* (2003). Yet as
he had shown in both *Before Sunrise* and *Waking Life,* he continued to cultivate his fascination with the nature of time and personal history, how people
grow and learn, and how we might change as we age.[2]
      Linklater, who has a fine appreciation of cinema history, had drawn some
inspiration for *Slacker* from the 1950 French film *La Ronde,* which linked
characters through their love affairs (Pierson 1995, p. 186). French cinema would again provide inspiration for him in making *Boyhood,* after he
recalled how *Mes Petites Amoureuses* (*My Little Loves,* 1974) told the story
of an adolescent boy over the course of time, yet Linklater felt the protagonist's aging process was too obviously artificial, and in order 'for [such a

story] to really work, you had to actually have everybody really age' (Paramount 2014).

Linklater thus envisioned an ongoing coherent project in the early 2000s that would follow a single child character through the twelve years of schooling that is typical of the American educational system – what he called 'the grid that we're sentenced to' – or roughly ages six to eighteen (Steinmetz 2014).

In 2002, he began shooting a film under the generic title of 'The 12-Year Project.' Its production would be audacious, and unprecedented: Linklater proposed to film for just a few days each year, in roughly one-year intervals, over the course of the protagonist's life, so that the audience would witness the character and his family aging through the course of the story.[3] The combination of the director's temporal and youthful enchantments thus motivated what would become the most concerted and comprehensive depiction of coming-of-age ever attempted in cinema history, defying the Bildungsroman tradition that is so often invested in sentimentality and marred by melodrama. By the time it debuted at the Sundance Film Festival in January of 2014, the film was called *Boyhood*.

This book is a study of the production, significance, context, and impact of that remarkable film. The first chapter takes up further issues of inspiration for Linklater as I examine other models of long-term filmmaking and situate the film within the long history of cinema's preoccupation with childhood life. The next chapter chronicles the development of the film from conception through its many years of shooting, covering germane aspects of Linklater's career up to and alongside *Boyhood*. I then move into an extensive critical evaluation of the film as a whole, examining each of its twelve 'years' and considering the stylistic and formal aspects of the film such as cinematography, editing, costuming, music, and particularly the script. The two chapters devoted to this analysis are divided by the protagonist's entry into his teenage years, and are further occupied by the film's narrative account of his development as a child within the structures of schooling, family, friendships, romance, sexuality, and society at large. The final chapter then describes the film's critical reception, box office, and awards before moving into a review of its many messages. Because the film is relatively recent, it has not yet attained the benefit of long-standing evaluation that would motivate a larger discussion of its value to cinema culture, and a narrative analysis such as I pursue here offers a more grounded (if still subjective) commentary on its content rather than an extensive theoretical or dogmatic exegesis, which all too often compromises academic work.

As I will elaborate, the protagonist of *Boyhood*, Mason (Ellar Coltrane), evolves through transitions from one year to the next that are often quite subtle, and some of which are detectable only by nuance. Rather than signaling the passage of time to his audience with obvious markers such as captions or title cards, Linklater shows Mason growing through changes in friendships, fashions, and attitudes, resulting in a canny statement on the often unpredictable ways in which young people come of age. Further, we watch how Mason's slightly older sister and his estranged parents grow and transform across the same period, each on occasion voicing shared frustrations with the vicissitudes of life, resulting in many profound (and sometimes unexpected) statements on learning, psychology, family, sexuality, and economics in the twenty-first century. As Boris Kachka (2014) concisely put it, Mason is 'a deer caught in the headlights of working-class, broken-home America.'

The America in which Mason aged from childhood to manhood was rife with historical change as well. When the story begins in early 2002, less than a year has elapsed since the shattering events of 9/11, the consequences of which Mason primarily hears through his left-wing father. The U.S. was by then already involved in an assured yet undeclared war in Afghanistan and within a few years would launch a far more dubious military attack on Iraq. Like many of his generation – who were slowly becoming known as Millennials – Mason grew up cynical and suspicious within the political atmosphere of the George W. Bush presidency, which was not alleviated by the election of Barack Obama in 2008. By then, the nation was in the grips of the Great Recession, which Mason observes through his working mother's difficulties with romantic partners, leading to upheavals in his education, housing, and social connections. American youth culture of the early twenty-first century was further impacted by the expansion of internet access, which was still something of a novelty when Mason started his schooling and was completely integrated into daily life by the time he graduated in 2013.

Boyhood would thus engage with more of the realistic conditions surrounding American youth than many higher-profile films of its period. While Hollywood remained content with making money on children's animation (*Hotel Transylvania* [2012], *Frozen* [2013], *Big Hero 6* [2014]) or teenage fantasies (the *Twilight* [2008–12] and *Hunger Games* [2012–15] films), and the indie market took on occasionally confrontational topics in *Standing Up* (2013), *Boy Meets Girl* (2014), and *Grandma* (2015), films about children *aging into* adulthood over the course of years were unknown. In that way, *Boyhood* fits no genre per se. It does not appropriate the heartening innocence of childhood so common to kids' stories dating back to Shirley Temple in the 1930s, nor does it exploit the salacious scandals of sexual experience so endemic to teen stories since the 1980s. *Boyhood* is undeniably a film about youth, yet freed from so many generic expectations put upon children's and teens' genres. This no doubt explains why Hollywood studios would avoid financing such a project, and why critics and audiences found the film so refreshing as an examination of childhood.

Linklater may have employed a unique method to depict Mason's continuing growth into adulthood, avoiding most signposts of annual maturation such as birthdays and anniversaries, yet we are given ample suggestions about his ongoing advancement, primarily through his varying living conditions, his shifting social circle, and the visible fluctuations of his hairstyle. Thus, we notice when the family relocates to different homes across southern Texas, we discern a few moments in cultural history, and we become aware of Mason's encroaching departure from boyhood itself as he moves toward high school graduation, leaving home, and going off to college. As Linklater (2014) has said, he 'wanted the movie to seem like the memory of a young life, just rolling through time,' and he captures that through this smooth progression of Mason on screen, void of many celebrated rituals that children have forced upon them, like holidays, vacations, and ceremonies. In fact, Mason has just one birthday in the story, his almost forgotten fifteenth, and Linklater even dodges Mason's actual graduation service.

Some of the directorial decisions about which events to record were essentially dictated by the shooting schedule. Linklater could only gather the cast and crew for a few days each year, and his budget was so low (merely $4 million by the time the production wrapped) that staging crowd events such as a graduation or winter scenes involving conspicuous weather variables would have been cost-prohibitive. Thus, Linklater usually portrayed just a few captured experiences in each year, from mundane moments of Mason attending school to a few more dramatic turns such as his mother leaving her second husband. This narrative method would indeed be rebellious within movie tradition, leading Gabe Klinger (n.d.) to adroitly claim that 'the hidden aim of *Boyhood* is to dismantle that convention in mainstream narrative cinema that characters' lives have to be defined by prescribed momentous events.'

Boyhood demonstrates the extent to which Linklater allows the quotidian growth of his protagonist to flourish on screen in subtle bursts of curiosity, arbitrary memories, and casual concerns about the meaning of life. At the same time, I argue that what Linklater makes appear so seamless and natural on screen is, in reality, a methodically designed and cogently analytical statement on the momentary grace of childhood and the evanescent nature of time itself.

Notes

1 Originally credited to an interview with Eric Kohn as first reported by Buder (2014) and reapplied in numerous articles thereafter.
2 Holly Willis (2014) provides an appreciative comparison of *Boyhood* with the three *Before* films – *Before Sunrise* (1995), *Before Sunset* (2004), and *Before Midnight* (2013) – in terms of temporal themes.
3 In an interview from 2010 while Linklater was still in production, he curiously remarked of *Boyhood*: 'I think time is sort of a lead character, if you wanted to get technical about it – the lead character of the movie.' See Johnson (2012), p. 148.

1 The child on screen
Capturing youth

Give me a child until he is seven and I will show you the man.

– Aristotle[1]

A true appreciation for the ingenuity and reach of *Boyhood* is best informed by understanding how it aligns with and deviates from the history of children's depictions in cinema, and by a comparison to other attempts at long-duration film productions, which themselves have an interesting place in cinema history. Because the childhood issue is more complex and lengthy, and connects with the subsequent chapter, I turn to the production issue first.

There are extremely few examples of long-duration single film productions in narrative cinema. At the same time, there are numerous examples of recurring characters played by the same actor over many different films, and in terms of young characters, one of the most famous is Andy Hardy, who was played by Mickey Rooney as a teenager beginning in 1937 with *A Family Affair* and continued for over a decade in fifteen films until 1947 with *Love Laughs at Andy Hardy*.[2] While these films featured returning characters and references to previous plotlines, they remained distinct productions such that each stood on its own. The same could be said of the films about young Antoine Doinel (Jean-Pierre Léaud), which French auteur François Truffaut began making in 1959 with *The 400 Blows* and revived across four more films until *Love on the Run* (1979), following this character from his early teens to his 30s.[3]

A closer parallel to the production of *Boyhood* was the *Harry Potter* series, which began as seven books released from 1997 to 2007 and was adapted into eight films, following the famous story of a boy who progresses through wizardry school across his teens. The first film appeared in 2001, just before production started on *Boyhood*, and continued with the same primary cast until 2011, a few years before shooting on *Boyhood* ended, prompting some critics to see a correlation between the two approaches.[4]

Kristin Thompson (2015) has even suggested that Linklater's conception of *Boyhood* may have arisen from the *Potter* phenomenon, which would have emerged by the time he thought of his own project (and he was at least so conscious of the connection that he included two *Potter* references within his story). Yet the parallel is disrupted on many levels, including the fact that novelist J.K. Rowling supplied the story for each film independent of production concerns, the story's otherworldly setting largely disregarded verisimilitude for contemporary youth, and four different directors made the films with budgets no less than $100 million each.

The *Potter* films also had the momentum of an established audience following the books as they were released, as well as the support of a major studio (Warner Bros.) that had the financial and technical means to ensure the sustenance of such an ambitious undertaking. Indeed, the liabilities and practicalities of mounting a multi-year production are daunting to say the least. Funding must first be secured, and while movie studios may have a horizon for taking a project from development to release over a few years, the true production time for most features is closer to a single year, with principal photography for the actors and key crew scheduled for usually no more than two months.[5] Any film that actually began with a plan covering many years before its release – during which a studio and ancillary investors must wait with uncertainty without any return on investment – would require an enormous leap of faith that corporate practices do not tolerate well.

Many variables could also wreak havoc on a very long production schedule, from environmental and technological changes to fluctuations in financial conditions for a studio to the limited availability of actors. Simply trying to maintain the continuity of actors' performances over a multimonth shoot is difficult enough, but over the course of years, changes in the corporeal aging of (particularly young) actors could disrupt the characters' appearances. Thus, casting actors for a long-duration production becomes especially critical, because those needed for key roles not only need to be available at different times over the course of years (which many Hollywood actors would not risk for fear of missing potential opportunities), but the director needs to have confidence in the cast to sustain their characters over extremely long intervals.[6] In the case of a film like *Boyhood*, which features two young children as leads, the casting is further based on intuition and hope, as neither actor had an established screen presence and/or proven acting talent.

Presumably the sole reason for deliberately attempting any long-duration film would be to demonstrate the passage of time, which previous movies had been content to represent through changes in makeup, costuming, cultural references, and the use of multiple cast members. With the advent of increasingly sophisticated digital effects, a film like *The Curious Case of Benjamin Button* (2008) was able to depict its title character across the vast expanse of his life with a single primary actor (Brad Pitt), whose face was digitally modified and added to different actors' bodies as he 'aged backwards' throughout the twentieth century.[7] Yet to achieve the authenticity of aging that Linklater envisioned for his project, and to stay within an indie budget that had no room for expensive effects (*Benjamin Button* cost over 37 times the amount of *Boyhood*), any digital depiction of the aging process would have been plainly unrealistic.

Realism is the domain of documentaries, many of which also eschew special effects for the sake of efficient storytelling dependent on veracity. Further, because documentaries are not typically bound by the complications of casting actors or the demands of a restricted shooting schedule, directors have often been able to film for many years in search of a complete testament to their given concern. This has been quite appreciable in some animal and nature documentaries, such as *Winged Migration* (2001), shot over three years; *Planet Earth* (2006), more than five years; and *Samsara* (2011), nearly five years. And some documentaries about humans have been shot over still longer periods, such as the famous British *Up* series that began with *Seven Up!* in 1964 and offered its latest installment with *56 Up* (2012). In this case, a movie crew has been visiting most of the same fourteen people every seven years for over 50 years now, documenting their progress through life beginning at age seven, and tacitly examining the influence of British class and social structures on the influence of citizens' development. While the *Up* series has obviously endured for considerably longer than the production of *Boyhood*, and has followed many more people, it is not limited to a coherent storyline.[8]

The unique magnitude of the *Boyhood* production can be further appreciated through an understanding of how few long-duration narrative films have been completed, many of which were not *planned* as such. For instance, Leni Riefenstahl's *Tiefland* (1954) began shooting in 1940 but was disrupted by WWII and not completed for fourteen years. The Indian film *Pakeezah* (1972) was similarly plagued by production delays when, after shooting sporadically for six years starting in 1958, work was adjourned due to personnel defections and not resumed until the early 1970s. The animated feature *The Thief and the Cobbler* was in various phases of shooting for 31 years starting in 1964, sustaining various funding dilemmas along the way, and even after its 1995 studio release, had three more edited versions released up to 2013. More recently, Michael Winterbottom did plan the production of *Everyday* (2012) to last for five years, shooting scenes for two-week periods once a year beginning in 2007, as the story chronicled changes in a family while a father serves time in prison. Although begun five years after the first filming for *Boyhood*, this British film can at least claim a similar production agenda.

Having established the distinctive design of *Boyhood*, Linklater would also offer an incomparable perspective on childhood due to the comprehensive detail of his story, since no film had previously attempted to depict a child for the duration of every single year in school.[9] In fact, since the early twentieth century, when most American children were done with schooling by their early teens, movies about children tended to focus their stories on one year of school or less, and despite the promotion of longer-term schooling (until the age of seventeen or eighteen) in the U.S. after WWII, extremely few films endeavored to depict more than a year of experience for their characters.

Before the 1930s, Hollywood featured relatively few child protagonists in movies at all. When major child stars began to emerge, such as Jackie Coogan (by the mid-1920s), Jackie Cooper (early 1930s), Shirley Temple (mid-1930s), and Mickey Rooney (late 1930s), they were almost always placed in scenarios with adult protagonists to ensure a wider audience appeal and to avoid concentrating on the child's ostensibly juvenile perspective. But the Great Depression elevated concerns about child welfare in the 1930s, and by the end of that decade, several films had emerged to address the experiences of primarily poor and troubled youth, which made for compelling drama and lucrative box office income. Many movies celebrated the gutsy nature of children overcoming the poverty and adversity of those years, often by adding musical elements that were newly appealing to the sound era. Films such as *Let's Sing Again* (1936), *One Hundred Men and a Girl* (1937), and *Babes in Arms* (1939) showed audiences that children, by being more focused on their families and simple pursuits of happiness, were a welcome antidote to the darker troubles that were more typical of films about adults at the time.

Alongside these cheerful cases, the studios were also discovering means of exploiting fears of youth, particularly in terms of delinquency. Cautionary tales appeared such as *Wild Boys of the Road* (1933) and *Reformatory* (1938), allegedly to forewarn youth against immorality while also enjoying the same sensational aspects of criminality that were making gangster films popular at the time. By the end of the decade, an entire series of films was built around this topic, beginning in 1937 with *Dead End*, which labored to show crime negatively although audiences were enthralled by its charismatic young characters who openly resent and combat the gentrification of their neighborhood. The film was such a hit that Warner Bros. developed more films around these so-called 'Dead End Kids,' and had an even bigger hit with *Angels with Dirty Faces* in 1939. The 'kids' grew into adulthood and carried on as the Bowery Boys in the 1940s, making dozens of films, with two actors, Huntz Hall and Leo Gorcey, going on to play their returning characters in over 40 different releases.

To be sure, by the 1930s Hollywood had promoted many characters played by the same actors across multiple films, such as Charlie Chaplin's famous Tramp in five features (and many more shorts) up to 1936, and Glenda Farrell's seven films as reporter Torchy Blane from 1937–39. Such a practice would also lead to the *Andy Hardy* films by the end of that decade, and like Hall and Gorcey, Mickey Rooney matured and aged over the course of his numerous reincarnations, and his stories retained most of the same characters, settings, and casts. To some extent, then, a slight precedent had been set by this point for movies following a young character into adulthood. The continuity of character and narrative that Linklater would later develop around *Boyhood*, however, would be far more linear and coherent.

In addition to facing the real-life dilemma of younger actors aging more visibly than older actors (Rooney's youthful appearance was aided by his short stature), Hollywood's interest in producing more films about youth would have the far thornier dilemma of adapting to the young population's changing interests and images. The 1940s were a relatively fallow period for movies about adolescent life as the industry focused on the war effort and recovery in the years thereafter, but in the 1950s, the nascent curiosities about juvenile delinquency that arose in the 1930s reawakened with abundance. By the middle of the 1950s, movie screens were filled with sensationalized stories from both major studios, such as the Warner Bros. landmark *Rebel Without a Cause* (1955), and the smaller but lucrative exploitation market, which rushed out titles that tapped into the trend of troubled youth, including *Teenage Rebel* (1956) and *Juvenile Jungle* (1958). These films appeared alongside youth culture's explosive interest in rock-and-roll music, which further symbolized the rebellion of independence that young people embraced during a decade that otherwise strove to present an image of domestic peace after the troubled war years.

Richard Linklater was born in 1960 as America was gaining an altogether new perspective on the young consumers, protesters, and artists that would have more influence in cultural events than any other generational group in the century. He would grow up watching the Vietnam War unfold on television while the student revolts of the late 1960s were overtaken by reassuring complacency in the disco era of his later teens. Linklater and his contemporaries witnessed an intriguing trajectory of youth representation at the movies throughout the course of their coming-of-age: Hollywood moved from sublimating teenage sex with sun-and-surf movies like *Beach Party* (1963) and *Beach Blanket Bingo* (1965) to celebrating outright druggy rebellion with *Wild in the Streets* (1968) and *Free Grass* (1969) to recalling simpler times before all that turmoil in *American Graffiti* (1973) and *Grease* (1978).

These two '70s hits were exceptions to the industry's otherwise derisory efforts to exploit the teenage audience during that decade, which resulted in forgettable fare such as *The Cheerleaders* (1973), *Massacre at Central High* (1976), and *Corvette Summer* (1978).

Indeed, the odd cycles of American youth cinema during the director's own formative years would find a certain realization in his formative features, made from the age of 31 to 36, the first four of which were single day-and-night narratives in the lives of (primarily) young people. *Slacker* (1991) was a mildly political response to the apathy that youth of the 1990s were accused of espousing; *Dazed and Confused* (1993) was a nostalgic tour of rebellious mid-1970s teens drifting through the drug culture of the time; *Before Sunrise* (1995) all but transferred the romantic longings of its characters into conversation; *SubUrbia* (1996) literally lined up disaffected young adults who find themselves in contemporary suspension without rebellion or nostalgia to relieve their anomie.

Curiously, Linklater's films about youth (which would later include *School of Rock* [2003] and *Bad News Bears* [2005] before *Boyhood*), would evade the trappings of the classic 1980s era of teen cinema characterized by sex romps (*Porky's* [1981], *Risky Business* [1983]), slasher series (*Friday the 13th* [1980], *A Nightmare on Elm Street* [1984]), and the sensitive films of John Hughes like *Sixteen Candles* (1984) and *The Breakfast Club* (1985). Such films, and the blockbuster success of family-friendly hits going back to *Star Wars* (1977), *Superman* (1978), and *E.T.* (1982), would revitalize the sagging Hollywood box office and convince the studios to return to a heavy investment in youth movies as they had done in the 1950s, though Linklater was not drawn to this impulse. He had spent much of the 1980s absorbing classic Hollywood and foreign films, as his generational cohort drifted out of the decade with scant career opportunities and a critical cynicism about the state of American culture.

So when Linklater emerged as a talent in the early 1990s, the atmosphere of disenchanted 'postmodern puberty' was ripe and ready for his forays into youth culture.[10] (See Figure 1.1.) After *Slacker*, further indie features proliferated to capitalize on the 20-somethings of Generation X who had been 1980s teenagers, including *Singles* (1992), *Clerks* (1994), *Empire Records* (1995), and *Reality Bites* (1994), starring future Linklater collaborator Ethan Hawke. The Hollywood studios had meanwhile moved away from young sexuality (fears of AIDS and the rise of teen pregnancies in the later 1980s had made the topic less entertaining) and as the horror genre was somewhat sustained through home video, the violence of slasher films was rerouted into real-life tales of teens confronting crime, particularly in the urban African American settings of *Boyz N the Hood* (1991), *Straight Out of Brooklyn* (1991), *Juice* (1992), and *Menace II Society* (1993).

Figure 1.1 Richard Linklater at a *Boyhood* premiere in 2014

As research by Considine (1985); Doherty (1988); Lewis (1992); Tropiano (2006); Driscoll (2011), and my own *Generation Multiplex* (2002, 2014) has shown, youth cinema developed into an established genre over the course of the late twentieth century. Klein's (2011) research on film cycles would further demonstrate that the 'teen film' fluctuates in output and popularity, as well as in its attention to different concerns and styles, which was clearly evident in its recurring rises and falls after the 1950s. The studios' preoccupations with music and dance trends, sexual exploration, and criminal commotion would continue to characterize many of the films about youth as cinema moved into the next century.

For instance, the horror genre was rejuvenated in the late 1990s with the success of knowing, self-critical killer chronicles such as *Scream* (1996), *I Know What You Did Last Summer* (1997), and *Cherry Falls* (2000). Teen sexuality returned with abundant concern alongside comfortable comedy: the former on display in *Kids* (1995), *Wild Things* (1997), and *The Virgin Suicides* (2000); the latter manifested in *American Pie* (1999), *But I'm a Cheerleader* (2000), and *Saved!* (2004). While the broader film industry enjoyed these demonstrative (if somewhat less lucrative) voyages through contemporary teen culture, Linklater had moved away from specific youth themes with his bigger-budget historical drama *The Newton Boys* (1998) and the more meditative *Waking Life* (2001) and *Tape* (2001). Given the adult and sometimes grave aspects of these films, the director looked as if he would abandon youth concerns altogether, and yet he was already planning *Boyhood* by 2001 and started the production in 2002.

Due to the extremely long duration of making *Boyhood*, any attempt to situate it within the generic cycles and patterns of Hollywood practices is difficult, and the nature of the film actually resists such positioning, so we must understand it as an artifact of evolution rather than of a specific era. After all, the contexts of social history and industrial activity can be rather diffuse in a movie that is written and revised over the course of twelve years. *Boyhood* became a film influenced by these contexts as Linklater and his actors progressed through that time, beginning in the post-9/11 atmosphere that young Mason hears referenced in his father's political rants. Other timely developments influence Mason's own development, although, true to childhood, none last for long. The *Harry Potter* phenomenon that infused the experiences of many children from 1997 to 2011 (while the books and films were first being released) is apparent in some of Mason's prepubescent activities but is never recalled later. His use of technology moves from the bulky tabletop computers of the early 2000s to handheld smartphones in the early 2010s. And even his father's ongoing inducement for Mason and Sam to be fervent Democrat activists – flaunted when he has them canvas for Barack Obama in 2008 – is gone by the time Mason is a jaded teenager and his father has taken to selling insurance and driving a minivan for the sake of his new wife and baby son.

The film thus implicitly shows how certain historical moments create backgrounds to Mason's life, yet are in many ways indifferent to it. The same applies to the place of *Boyhood* within the genre of youth cinema, because it enlists very few of the generic conventions that characterize teen movies (in terms of stock characters, dramatic conflicts, or appeals to adventure). Hollywood trends nonetheless continued to progress during the years the film was in development, none of which had any particular impact on its production. For instance, aside from the two *Harry Potter* references, we see no evidence of the turn toward supernatural stories in teen cinema, which became abundant by the end of the 2000s with the *Twilight* pentalogy that started in 2008.

A similar indifference applies to the film's address of identity politics during an era in which young people became pressured to abandon binary and restrictive labels (female/male, black/white, poor/rich) as they began exploring fluidity in demographic categories that they were simultaneously being encouraged to acknowledge (gender, sexuality, race, ethnicity, nationality, class, education) like never before. Mason thus has the privilege of his American white male heterosexuality, yet even as a working-class kid, he is not brought to confront his place in society within these terms, nor does he consciously classify himself within the various collective ranks that so many young people have been compelled to adopt and refine over generations. Mason denies the facile branding that has been put upon so many young protagonists (hooligan, punk, jock, goth, nerd, rebel, stoner, dude), and for that matter, he is clearly detached from much of popular culture by the time he is a teen, not embracing any particular musical styles, not enamored of particular artists, and not aligned with the fussy zeitgeist of the early 2010s.

Boyhood could thus be released in 2014 with a protagonist and a story that were not beholden to current conditions in order to demonstrate relevance. The relevance of the film, and Mason's experiences within it, lay in its inclusive quality of youthful experiences that are not mired in passing cultural customs. Mason may be a child of the early twenty-first century, but in so many ways he is representative of children across generations since the start of cinema, and *Boyhood* itself is the result of every youth film that had come before: a sincere summation of the genre's numerous interests rendered in a sui generis style entirely its own.

Notes

1   There are competing attributions for this quotation: first to Aristotle (384–322 BC), and then revised by St. Francis Xavier (1506–1552), more commonly translated as, 'Give me a child until he is seven and I will give you the man.' This is the assertion that is a declared rationale in the *Up* series.

2   Rooney would play the Andy Hardy character one more time, as an adult, in *Andy Hardy Comes Home* (1958).

3   The other Doinel films were *Antoine and Colette* (1962), *Stolen Kisses* (1968), and *Bed & Board* (1970). Truffaut unfortunately died in 1984, so we will never know how he might have continued Antoine's life into middle age, but unlike *Boyhood,* his ongoing tales of the character had been unplanned and shot in indiscriminate intervals.

4   A widely circulated parody trailer by Slate, *Potterhood*, humorously confirmed the parallels between the films. See Jagernauth (2014).

5   While stories of unbearably long shooting schedules in Hollywood have often been apocryphal, various sources claim that the 1999 Stanley Kubrick film *Eyes Wide Shut* had the longest continuous principal photography, with a shoot lasting over 15 months. See Nicholson (2014).

6   Linklater knew of the 'De Havilland' law that resulted from actress Olivia de Havilland's contract dispute with her studio in the 1940s, which forbids contracts beyond seven years. This necessitated contract renewals for much of his cast and crew. See Thompson (2015).

7   A detailed explanation of the process is available in Seymour (2009).

8   Other *Up* series began in seven-year intervals in nations such as the United States (1991), Soviet Union (1991), Japan (1992), and South Africa (1992), and a new British series began in 2000 with *7Up 2000.* Lesser-known examples of extreme long-duration documentary filmmaking include the work of noted

Australian director Gillian Armstrong, who, beginning with *Smokes and Lollies* in 1976, began documenting women starting in their adolescence and revisiting them each decade, most recently in *Love, Lust & Lies* (2009). The Czech Republic film *René* (2008) was filmed over the course of 20 years. More remarkably, and predating the *Up* series, *The Children of Golzow* began shooting in East Germany in 1961 and continued production across 20 installments for 46 years, with none more than four years apart, until concluding in 2007.

9 *Billy Madison* (1995) does follow the adult title character as he repeats his schooling from first to twelfth grades to qualify for an inheritance, but quickly passes over his middle school years and depicts the whole process taking place in the space of a mere few months.

10 See my analysis (Shary 1999) of 1990s movies emblematic of this atmosphere. Specific to Linklater and the postmodern, see Harrod (2010).

2 An audacious adventure
Making the life of Mason

The film of tomorrow appears to me then, to be more personal than a novel; it will be individual and autobiographical, like a confession, or an intimate diary.

– François Truffaut (1957)

Before Richard Linklater would embark on the path to *Boyhood*, his early adulthood had already been an interesting journey. He was a Texas boy himself since his birth in Houston in 1960, and many aspects of his upbringing would inform his development of Mason over 40 years later.[1] Linklater's father was an insurance agent (as Mason Sr. becomes), and his parents divorced when he was seven years old, leading him to spend weekends with his father after moving away with his mother (and two older sisters) to the small town of Huntsville, a little over an hour from Houston (Lowenstein 2009, p. 3). Just as Mason's mother in *Boyhood* endures multiple boyfriends and becomes a professor after her second divorce, Linklater's mother became a professor after her divorce and had 'a succession of new boyfriends and stepfathers,' although young Rick indulged his growing passion for movies during his visits to his father back in the city (Dawidoff 2015).

While he did not have youthful aspirations to become a movie director, he did pride himself on his creative writing skills as early as elementary school. In high school, he has said, 'I had an influential English teacher in my third year [and she] actually showed us *Battleship Potemkin* [1925] and we had to analyze it. So I started thinking about film a little bit' (Lowenstein 2009, p. 4). Otherwise, he has characterized his high school years as 'some existential teenage crisis' that did not impede his ability to be an athlete and chase girls (Lowenstein 2009, p. 4). Like Mason Jr., he went on to a Texas state college, Sam Houston State University, where in 1980 he qualified for a baseball scholarship (an experience that would inspire his 2016 film

Everybody Wants Some!!), and there he enjoyed English courses that featured movie screenings.[2] However, a heart ailment meant that he could not
continue athletically, and even though he could have retained his scholarship, he dropped out in 1982.

The future auteur's more fruitful film education would occur over the
next few years, as he went to work on an offshore oil rig, saving his earnings
and spending his spare time watching movies at Houston cinemas (Stone
2013, p. 16). In 1984, he moved to the city that would become his lifelong home, Austin, having invested in super-8 filmmaking equipment and
embarking on an ambition to see three movies every day, in theaters or
through the increasingly popular medium of home video. During this time,
Linklater took two inspiring film studies courses at Austin Community College, and befriended filmmaker Lee Daniel, with whom he would found the
Austin Film Society in the fall of 1985 (Stone 2013, p. 17). This endeavor
gave him a platform for screening a wide range of films to an appreciative
public, as well as further connections to the local art scene.[3]

The budding director completed his first short film with Daniel, *Woodshock*, in 1985, documenting a local music festival on classically grainy film
stock, while the duo continued running the film society through featuring
a bevy of European films. By the time of his next film, *It's Impossible to
Learn to Plow by Reading Books* (1988), an 85-minute meandering meditation shot on super-8 featuring Linklater as the primary character, his innate
concerns about time and change within humdrum existence were already
evident.[4] The narrative follows Linklater's nameless college student on his
travels as he spends undefined intervals silently searching for nothing in
particular.[5] There was no commercial capacity in the plotless feature, yet it
was clearly a formative exercise for the promising cineaste, suggesting the
fascination he would cultivate in further projects about aimless experiences,
which (as we know) otherwise characterize much of life. His appreciation
for the post-war European cinema aesthetic that often emphasized experience over adventure, or emotion over action, and his attention to small but
potentially significant moments that cinema could so exquisitely celebrate
and preserve, would become the foundation for the film that first brought
him notoriety, *Slacker* (1991).

After this breakthrough, which demonstrated Linklater's affinity for
dialogue, his narrative and philosophical preoccupations would be on full
display across another six features over the next decade. By 2001, having
made somewhat conventional features such as *Before Sunrise* (1995) and
The Newton Boys (1998), Linklater returned to more experimental methods
in *Waking Life* and *Tape* (both 2001). The former used specialized computer
animation played over live-action ruminations on consciousness by Linklater characters who were familiar from his *Slacker* roles, and the latter

was a real-time confrontation between three old college friends confined to a solitary motel room, shot on the emerging medium of high-definition video. Against the varied if coherent work he had made to that point, and after becoming a father in 1994, his interests in time, youth, and the significance of small moments motivated him to design the twelve-year project that would become *Boyhood.*

Linklater conceived of the idea for *Boyhood* in mid-2001, and after calling it 'The 12-Year Project' during production, the film was tentatively titled *12 Years* until *12 Years a Slave* coincidentally appeared in 2013, forcing a name change (Lewis 2014b). According to Nicole Sperling, 'He was searching for a way to make a movie about childhood but was struggling to isolate one moment that defines it. . . . He'd grown up a child of divorce, moving around a lot, and was then still a relatively new father' (2014, pp. 31–32). And as Linklater would say himself, this project 'became a 12-year journey about coming to grips with my own childhood, while also understanding parenting' (Sperling 2014, p. 32). Cinematic and literary attempts to render long passages in a life over time had been tried before, but Linklater's vision would represent an unparalleled attempt to cast Hollywood actors and relative unknowns for a production schedule that had never been undertaken. The film would thus require an enormous leap of faith by its financiers, and the continuing commitment of its cast and crew.

Linklater's casting of his four lead roles would be an understandably delicate and deliberate process. He first collaborated with casting director Anne Walker-McBay to bring in the principal players, before bringing in Beth Sepko as his year-over-year casting director to fill out minor and sporadic roles (Peikert 2014). He knew he needed some 'bankable' names for the two adults in order to facilitate funding, and for Mason's father, the director called on his most reliable star, Ethan Hawke, who had already been featured in *Before Sunrise, The Newton Boys*, and *Tape* (and given a brief scene in *Waking Life*). The actor was also in the ideal age range of his early thirties, appropriate to be the father to Mason and his eight-year-old sister Samantha when shooting began in 2002. Hawke's father had been a Texan in the insurance business who got married a second time, a real-life connection to the character that inspired his role (Whipp 2015).

In casting Samantha, Linklater again went with the familiar, and more specifically the familial, by enlisting the eight-year-old girl he knew best, his daughter Lorelei. Even though the younger Linklater could not know her adolescent destiny, the director was clearly relying on an anticipated authenticity in filming his daughter under his guidance throughout her childhood.

For what would turn out to be the most dramatic role in the story, that of Mason's mother Olivia, the director sought out Patricia Arquette, who would be 34 at the start of production. As she said in reflecting on her decision to take the part:

> I already had a [thirteen-year-old] son by that point. And I'd already seen how fast it'd gone. I'd already had the little goings away that happen along the life of a child: your first day of school, the first time you let them sleep at someone else's house. All of those little moments that you go through as passages together. And I'd seen how fast that it happened with my son, and to me, it was the most beautiful thing I'd ever experienced – and difficult. So to see that happen in a movie seemed like an incredible idea.
>
> (Labrecque 2014b)

The subtle, studied nuances of Olivia's development over the course of the narrative would provide the film with an emotional foundation that few stories about coming-of-age could ever muster. Linklater was particularly in tune with Olivia as a mother since he based her on his own, who similarly went through divorce, earned her graduate degree, became a teacher, and had trouble with different men while raising her kids as a single mom (Whipp 2015). As with Hawke's sympathy for his character, Arquette had a mother who went back to school and became a teacher later in life, and audiences and critics were quick to recognize how much the actress brought to her experience, which led to her numerous awards for the part, including the Best Supporting Actress Oscar.

For his protagonist, Linklater would take the biggest risk of all, because he needed to find a six-year-old boy who would fit his existing vision (which was primarily informed by his own childhood characteristics) and furthermore, whose parents would agree to sign off on a contract with their son's best interests in mind. In fact, the contracts themselves would require faith beyond their legal stipulations: under California law, no one can be placed under a contract for more than seven years, and thus at least one renewal of the agreement would need to be signed again during production (Thompson 2015). The director set up open calls for young actors in Austin, outside of the usual agent-driven casting search, because Linklater wanted a performer who lived in the area. As he explained to Jeff Labrecque (2014a):

> We're low budget, so we couldn't have flown him in from far away. It would've made him a tougher collaborator to not have him nearby [for the next twelve years]. Because I knew I wanted to be in his life a little more and really be a family member, and be able to call him up and go get lunch.

Labrecque likened the audition to a playdate, with Linklater asking the boy candidates general questions in an effort to know them, rather than having them recite lines from the script (which did not yet exist). Linklater appreciated that Ellar Coltrane not only looked like the offspring of Hawke and Arquette, but his parents were artists whom he anticipated would be sympathetic to the long creative process their son would endure.[6] Further, Linklater found in the boy a certain essence he had been seeking:

> A lot of child actors try too hard. They try to be cute or whatever, because that's what's worked for them. He was very real. He didn't care what you thought about him, he was very passionate about music and stories and movies. Not *too* cool, but you know, a cool guy. He seemed like the better angel to follow, in the long term. I felt, that's the more thoughtful, interesting guy. Because that's who he was. He was kind of this ethereal, interesting kid.
>
> (Labrecque 2014a)

Coltrane, who was being homeschooled while he did some theater acting and had filled a small part in the Austin indie *Lone Star State of Mind* (2002), took to the production with the cool confidence that Linklater saw in him from the start.[7] The director got to know the boy through his artwork and taste in music, and he even set up a temporary family arrangement for Arquette to play mother to Coltrane and Lorelei, as she explained:

> Before we started filming, Rick had me take the kids for the weekend. They had a sleepover with me. We did arts and crafts. I cooked them breakfast in the morning. We bonded like that.
>
> (Steinmetz 2014)

The production of *Boyhood* then took place over 39 total shooting days, which is actually typical for many indie features, but those shoots were spread out over more than 4,000 days in real life, which was, of course, the radical difference.[8] This meant that enormous stretches of time would elapse between events for characters with coherent histories, thus placing a certain pressure on the actors to maintain some level of continuity in their performances despite significant changes in their lives, and it further placed a similar obligation on Linklater and his crew to maintain technical continuities for the duration.

Perhaps the biggest threat in that regard was the movie industry's encroaching rejection of film stock as a shooting medium, which had been standard since the earliest days of cinema in the 1890s. By the early 2000s, an increasing number of productions, particularly in the lower-budget independent realm, were moving toward less-expensive high-definition digital video, and certainly by the time of production on *Boyhood*, the use of video was an option. Linklater, who had recently worked with digital video on *Waking Life* and *Tape* in 2001, nonetheless committed to the more familiar format of film stock when he started *Boyhood* in 2002, knowing he was somewhat gambling that the older medium would persist for the length of production. As he said from the start,

> I want the film to look like *one* film, not different technologies or different looks for twelve years. I want this to be seamlessly dissolving from one year into the next, just people subtly aging.
>
> (Dunaway and Wood 2014)

Little did he realize what a calculated risk he was taking then: by the time *Boyhood* wrapped production in 2013, many movies were being shot on digital video (including major studio projects like *Oz: The Great and Powerful, World War Z*, and *Gravity*, which won the Best Cinematography Oscar that year), and at the time the film premiered the next year, roughly 90% of all movie screens in America were projecting digital images, not film (Alexander and Blakely 2014). Ashley Clark (2014) even suggested that Linklater's use of film in the digital era 'operates as a quiet lament for a dying medium.' In an unintended yet parallel irony, Mason ages in the movie as the mode representing him is aging out of existence.

Beyond the technical realm, continuity would also be a vital concern in conveying the evolving story, from costuming to sets to vehicles and other props. Linklater could rely on the sartorial connections made over the years by his costumer Kari Perkins, who would persuade cast members to use their own clothes or buy appropriate working class attire at local Goodwill stores (Steinmetz 2014). Set photographer Matt Lankes also provided an extensive visual record of the cast and settings each year, from which Linklater could plan certain features in the shooting of subsequent year's scenes.[9] The director had to make more advanced allowances for significant developments in the actors' appearances – particularly hair styles, such as asking Coltrane to let his mop top grow long before a traumatic cut in the fourth year – and in one of the most visible cases, a character's choice of car would undergo a vital shift. Mason Sr.'s 1968 GTO, a muscle car that embodies his immature masculine imprudence with its lack of seatbelts and excessive exhaust resonance, was actually Linklater's personal vehicle, which he had already used in *Slacker* and *Dazed and Confused* (1993).[10] While the car suited the reluctant young father's role, after Mason Sr. remarries and has another baby later in life, he sells off the symbol of rebellion to purchase a sensible nondescript minivan.

The financial matters that affected the characters in *Boyhood* would in some ways resemble the funding of the film itself. After all, Linklater was not a blockbuster role model despite enjoying modest success with his films throughout the production period, particularly *School of Rock* in 2003. He began by looking for funding at large, and then approached the independent IFC Films, which had grown from the Independent Film Channel, both of which were owned by AMC Networks, the conglomerate that also owned the AMC and Sundance television channels. The president of IFC Films, Jonathan Sehring, became a key ally, since the company had supported *Waking Life* and *Tape*, and he agreed to a modest allocation of about $200,000 for each year of shooting (Steinmetz 2014). By the time the film was complete, the total budget would reach $4 million, a humble figure for a film about working-class characters, even within the indie market, and more so compared to studio films that typically spend over $100 million for stories about more glamorous figures.[11]

Linklater himself would make a savvy and rather risky move with his own financial connection to the film. During negotiations with AMC, he brought in his trusted lawyer John Sloss, who made a deal so that IFC Films would allow the director to maintain partial ownership of the copyright, an unconventional arrangement. However, as Tatiana Siegel (2014) explained, 'Unlike a typical deal that offers a percentage of profits – or "points" – so a director shares in the success but has no control over the movie's future, Linklater's pact gave him a say in where and how the film is released.' The contract gave Linklater an influence in marketing and the ability to eventually sell his stake in the film rather than earning likely lower royalties in perpetuity. The compromise was that the director would forsake his guaranteed fee up front, which had typically been well over a million dollars, so he was clearly gambling on the film's success. This strategy also indicated a certain confidence: Linklater was not only risking a lower return overall, but his payday would be deferred for over a decade, during which he would be systematically (if very slowly) investing increasing amounts of his time and effort. Clearly he had faith in his vision from the start.

Thus, with Sehring providing financing and Sloss instilling legal muscle, the two were designated producers on the film along with Linklater. Cathleen Sutherland, who began as the film's production manager, came on as another producer (her first time in such a role) during the second year, and she took on the laborious coordination of more than 350 crew positions on the film (Grosz 2014). As Sutherland thus worked at maintaining the tricky continuity of the production for twelve years and Linklater revised his story ideas and scene plans, Sehring was mentally hedging his bet on the film, assuming that if 'something goes wrong, we'll have three or four years of footage and we'll do it as a web series, or a TV thing' (Fleming 2014).

Linklater and Sutherland had reasonable worries that something could indeed go wrong, such as a catastrophic event that would derail the production altogether. Keeping a calm demeanor, the director envisioned much more manageable changes that he could work into the story, like Coltrane arriving to shoot in the ninth year with painted nails. Rather than having the actor merely remove the polish, Linklater worked the change into Mason's nonchalance about appearance and his stepfather's concerns about gender roles. In terms of possibly devastating changes or the loss of a principal cast member, Linklater noted:

> There wasn't a plan B. I never remember thinking in those terms. It was like we were all going to do it, or we weren't. If someone fell out or we all looked at each other and said, 'Hey, this isn't working and this isn't fun, let's bail,' I would pay IFC back. But it went in the right direction. The film gained momentum year by year. It didn't lose spirit, it gained it.
>
> (Labrecque 2014a)

Contrary to appearances and assumptions, Linklater writes his scripts quite consciously in advance, and then further develops the movie's dialogue with his primary cast members (Kohn 2014).[12] Thus, most events in *Boyhood* were planned before shooting, and Linklater encouraged his actors' input in staging their scenes, as Coltrane explains:

> Especially as I got older, I became a pretty direct part of writing the dialogue – which most of the actors were. He would have the framework of the scene and we would just have conversations, and that would become the dialogue. I never had to think about getting in character, and that's really one of Rick's magic tricks. You don't really know it, and then suddenly you *are* the character. It's incredible.
>
> (Mechanic 2014)

Principal photography for *Boyhood* began in late summer 2002 and lasted until August 2013, when Linklater and editor Sandra Adair began the postproduction process with supervisor Laura Yates, who had recently worked with Linklater on the completion of *Before Midnight*, which appeared that same year. While any other film of nearly three hours in length could easily take over 100 editors and technicians to complete over the course of many months, the trio worked with merely a dozen credited staff in the editorial department (Adair had used only four assistant editors during the lengthy production), and together they completed a release print of the film for screening at the Sundance Film Festival in January 2014, less than five months later.[13] This was possible because Adair had worked with Linklater on preliminary edits of each section within the film across the previous twelve years, as she explained:

> Every year, I would work for three to four weeks editing that year's material. For the first few years, we wouldn't really worry about attaching one segment to the next, but once we got down the line about four or five years, we started making an assembly of all the years [up to that point]. And each year after that, when that year's segment was edited, we'd attach it to the tail of the other years.
>
> (Alter 2014)

Thus, as Adair would add, 'we had the movie pretty finely edited by the time we attached the most recent material' (Alter 2014). By the time *Boyhood* would make its debut at Sundance, this film that had been in production for nearly twelve years, during which Mason and Coltrane grew from young boys to young men, was ready to depict its unique coming-of-age story that would captivate audiences and garner essentially universal critical acclaim.

Notes

1 In addition to the autobiographical aspects detailed throughout this volume, Linklater elaborates on the numerous other elements of *Boyhood* that he appropriated from his own youth in the Criterion Collection DVD (2016a) audio commentary.
2 For the story of Linklater's baseball career, as well as a picture of him on the Sam Houston State team, see Schallenberg (2016).
3 Emanuel Levy (1999) examines Linklater's early films in relation to their Austin environs.
4 *It's Impossible to Learn to Plow by Reading Books*, along with *Woodshock*, is contained on the Criterion Collection DVD (2004) of *Slacker*. In the audio commentary, Linklater cites as an early influence the Belgian structuralist filmmaker Chantal Akerman.
5 Cult director Monte Hellman (2004), director of *Two-Lane Blacktop* (1971), describes his response to receiving a videotape copy of *It's Impossible to Learn to Plow by Reading Books* from Linklater in 1989, to which he responded with such enthusiasm that Linklater used Hellman's letter to raise money for *Slacker.*
6 The actor's full name was Ellar Coltrane Salmon until he 'decided to use his middle name as his last name professionally when the film wrapped as he became wary of attaching his family's name to the movie,' according to Lewis (2014a).
7 Linklater had grown comfortable enough with Coltrane to give him a small role in his 2006 film *Fast Food Nation*.
8 On June 23, 2014, Kohn (in Buder 2014) quoted Linklater: 'We started this film 4,207 days ago. We think that's the longest production in history.'

9 Many of these production images have been collected in Lankes (2014).
10 Dargis (2014) points out that this GTO is 'the same model of masculine cool that rumbles through 'Two-Lane Blacktop,' one of Mr. Linklater's favorite movies.'
11 For detailed financial information on *Boyhood*, see Nash (2017).
12 Former cast members also describe developing scripted dialogue with Linklater in Dunaway and Wood (2014).
13 These details are available on the Internet Movie Database listings for the film: www.imdb.com/title/tt1065073/?ref_=fn_tt_tt_1.

3   Understanding *Boyhood*

The child becomes a teenager

Youth / is the ability to be / single-minded as water caressing a stone / and
ambidextrous as the wind / ringing all its bells / at the same time.
— Richard Shelton (1982)

There is a persuasive impulse to analyze *Boyhood* in chronological order,
given how it is so assiduously attentive to a progressive order of events.
Thus the following analysis will, for the most part, examine the film in the
order it unfolds, while taking opportunities to elaborate on specific topics
as they become germane. Just as there is no unifying method to the film
aside from its attention to Mason's evolution, I am not enforcing a specific
approach to understanding the film, which asks to be appraised through
multiple lenses of evaluation.

Thus, as I proceed to discuss each of the twelve intervals that make up
the film, I will alternately call attention to the story, acting, cinematography, editing, music, costuming, and messages. This last topic may inevitably be the most contentious, as any interpretation of movies is malleable
and contextual, influenced by the time of the film's creation as well as
its reception, and certainly worthy of question in relation to the filmmak-
ers' intentions and the audiences' perceptions. In the case of a film like
Boyhood, the incredibly long production duration and the verisimilitude
of its approach to childhood create a rich opportunity to consider social
contexts that changed over time as the film was made. Certainly there
are many interpretations to be made of this film, yet against the film's
supposed neutrality, a network of compelling statements emerge about
boyhood and its vicissitudes, the power of family dynamics in shaping
who children become as adults, and in general, the culture of American
youth in the post-9/11 era.

Youth culture was certainly in the throes of ongoing upheavals during
this era. After the menacing terrorist attacks in 2001 left American children

traumatized by the threat of harm from without, the ensuing news of constant combat in the Middle East gave them an impression of their nation in an endless state of war. At the local level, youth had become accustomed to news of school shootings in recent years, which reached epidemic proportions in the decade before 9/11 (over 200 children shot in 55 incidents), leading to 'lockdown' drills implemented by many administrators. Alas, this morbid trend persisted with mass shootings (four or more murdered) at elementary schools in 2006 and 2012, high schools in 2005 and 2014, and universities (six times since 2001).[1]

This culture of violence permeated children's entertainment with the increasing promotion of sadistic video games, as the expansion of the internet also gave youth unprecedented access to information and communication that adult authorities could barely monitor. Children's activities thus simultaneously acquired visibility – and exploitability – especially in the form of social networks that gained traction throughout the early part of the century. Suddenly children with computer access could proclaim themselves as individuals around the world, while local friends and rivals could also lay claim to their messages and images with no limit on critical commentary, giving rise to 'cyberbullying' and its pernicious effects.

And soon after these developments relocated the social pressures of school to home, young people began to literally embrace these communicative tensions with their bodies through the expansion of the smartphone in the late '00s, which further burdened the population with a perceived need for ceaseless connection. Along the way, children were further targeted by a media industry eager to elevate them to adult status as consumers, which the internet only made easier through its proliferation of customized marketing.[2] While some cultural changes showed progress toward tolerance, such as the election of an African American president (2008) and the legalization of same-sex marriage (2013), the political prominence of youth was largely diminished because their characteristic causes – the environment, gender and racial equality, and education – continued to be treated with desultory lip service by most adult leaders.

Given this specific atmosphere in which the protagonist of *Boyhood* lives, any critic may take issue with the film for the ambition of its ambiguous title, which is certainly assumptive in the implied claim of its name; after all, this is but *one* boyhood, one of millions going on in America at the same time. Mason cannot possibly represent the diversity of identities that all the boys across the country embodied across the years of the story, in terms of demographics such as race, sexuality, class, or religion, nor in terms of location, health, psychology, or circumstance. The closest Mason comes to representational status is his statistical normality – the plurality of American boys during the time of production were white, heterosexual, working class, and had one sibling (Livingston 2015) – but then he emerges as having artistic ambitions uncommon to most boys, and a disinterest in sports that is equally uncommon.

We could further compare the average age at which American boys first take on paying jobs, earn a driver's license, lose their virginity, or achieve other landmarks of adolescence, yet Linklater dutifully dodges any celebration of moments that deliberately signify Mason's 'growth,' even omitting his high school graduation to focus on the family party afterward. As we come to understand about Mason while the film unspools, he has no intention of being representative, and he is plainly aware of his life being a singular experience. The film suggests that regardless of identity markers, American children at large go through the common evolution of schooling, aging into adulthood along the way, and trying to find their way afterward. The mundane momentum of daily experience, our collective inability to comprehend the significance of our lives as we live them, and the recognition that present time is truly the only time within our reach, are the themes that give *Boyhood* its salient universality.

A practical breakdown of the film's sections is most helpful in understanding the progression of its story. Across its complete running time of 2 hours, 45 minutes, and 15 seconds, Linklater presents his twelve segments corresponding to different times in Mason's life without any textual labels on screen to indicate the transition from one year to another.[3] In fact, the script published by Linklater gives no indications of divisions between years and rarely provides information that definitively indicates Mason's age, school grade, or the current year. This results in a distinct uncertainty between the years we witness, and further masks the inconsistency in shooting patterns of the actual production. Some shoots were done during summer seasons, but various factors required that the twelve shooting sessions be staggered at uneven intervals, so we are primarily directed to annual transitions by the characters' changing appearances, particularly hairstyles. (The initial DVD release from Paramount [2014] was not divided into annual sections, although the later Criterion Collection DVD [2016] did link its chapters to each year of the story.)

I should say that Linklater himself could have reservations about this kind of scrupulous articulation of the events in a film meant to show a boy's life simply advancing without regard to demarcations in years, yet this dissection of time in the film reveals his careful decision-making in the production process, which itself developed as he worked on the film for so long. We can see through this chronology how Linklater makes his case for the coherence of life by obscuring denotative temporal elements in telling Mason's story, and how efficiently he is able to convey the very amorphous process of growth that characterizes childhood itself.

Each section of the sequential commentary that follows notes the time code from the Criterion DVD (with the zero mark on the disc just before the film credits), based on the start and end of shots corresponding to those sections, and enumerates scene changes within the story.

Year one [0:01:00–0:11:19]

Mason Evans Jr. is about six years old in first grade during May 2002.[4] The story action takes place over several indeterminate days.

1 Olivia picks up Mason at school, then drives him home asking about his behavior.
2 Mason plays with his friend Tommy, until Sam calls him to dinner [later that day].
3 Mason sees Olivia's boyfriend Ted drop by their house [that evening].
4 Olivia reads a *Harry Potter* book to Mason and Sam in bed [that night].
5 Mason gets out of bed to see Olivia arguing with Ted [later that night].
6 Sam taunts Mason by singing a song, and Olivia yells at them [the next morning].
7 Mason and Tommy look at women in a lingerie catalog [could be another day].
8 Mason contemplates a dead bird [later that day].
9 Olivia tells the kids over dinner that they're moving to Houston [that evening].
10 Mason asks Olivia if she still loves his father [could be another night].
11 Mason helps Olivia paint over walls while Sam talks on the phone [another day].
12 The three leave their house with Sam whining [later that day].
13 The kids taunt each other on the way to Houston [later that day].
14 The family drives up to their new apartment [that evening].

The short opening credits [0:00:00–0:00:59] play under the introductory chords of Coldplay's 2000 song 'Yellow,' which Linklater chose as a representative hit from that era.[5] The initial lyrics, 'Look at the stars, look how they shine for you,' play just as the image cuts from a soothing blue sky of clouds to a close-up of young Mason, late in his first grade year, gazing up at that sky in pensive repose. Jonathan Lethem (2016) remarked on this opening, 'Like a cloud, the film before us both invites our ceaseless projections and brushes them off.' At this moment, Mason could be thinking about space or earth, but as he soon reveals to Olivia when she approaches, he has made a discovery about the way wasps are formed when 'you flick a rock into the air just right.' This lack of scientific accuracy is easily dismissed by his mother, who will soon enough explain her concerns about such daydream-ing (his teacher is concerned that he is 'still staring out the window all day'), a creative quality so often squelched by systems of schooling and adulthood that deny its inspiring potential.[6]

From the first scene, Mason faces a challenge to his view of life, as Olivia will further inquire why he placed rocks in his classroom's pencil sharpener. His explanation is entirely rational – 'I thought if we could sharpen pencils, maybe we could sharpen rocks' – because he is seeking sharp rocks to add to his arrowhead collection. Mason's creative impulses and energies will be much further negotiated as the film proceeds, and his curiosities to under-stand wasps foreshadow the inquisitive nature he will bring to his whole life.

The eyeline match to Mason's perspective in the first edit is worth noting further, because while we are welcomed from the start to survey his life, we are not often privileged to his actual sight. The opening credit background shot is thus one of the significant point-of-view shots in the film, even as Linklater thereafter engages us primarily in studying Mason and his environ-ment, often diligently avoiding the narrative trappings of POV (and always eschewing voiceover) that would constrain and 'fix' our understanding of what he sees and feels. Linklater, and his cinematographers Lee Daniel and Shane Kelly, also tend to avoid the use of typical establishing shots, which are used to set up the characters and contents of a scene. His editor Sandra Adair generally minimized insert shots as well, which cover gaps in action or time, choosing instead to have each new scene begin with relevant action, and then usually maintaining the duration of that action within one location for the length of the entire scene. This technique provides the story with more complete moments of Mason's experience and also conditions the audience to accept a rather languid pace for the story. Further, numerous jump cuts will be used during significant transitions in time and space, which would be quite disorienting in conventional narratives, but here become part of the audience's experience in 'sampling' these scenes from a boy's life.

Consider the movement of the first scene, and its next transition into the further sequence. We literally move with Mason, away from school and into his mother's car as they drive home, and this sense of propulsion will accom-pany Mason for much of the narrative. We will often see him in vehicles: for most of the film, he is being driven by his mother or father, until his later teen years when he at last gains the ability to take himself to new places, an undeniable liberation for many youth. Before he is sixteen, though, he must be carried and escorted, reinforcing his lack of self-determination, more so in his younger years when he is relegated to the back seat.

This first trip with Mason takes us across his unnamed hometown, where he later meets up with his long-haired friend Tommy (Elijah Smith), with whom he rides bicycles and delights in spray painting a large if awkward 'X' on the wall of a tunnel. We again behold Mason's creative impulse, and will later see his typographical work on display during eighth grade when he displays a large 'graffiti painting' in his bedroom. This moment of expression is nonetheless disrupted by the introduction of his sister Samantha, calling out for him to come home to dinner. Like many younger children, Mason lives under the management of his older sibling, who will occasionally taunt and provoke him throughout the rest of his life. Sam will continue to dismiss her authority over Mason, as well as much of the responsibility that comes with it; she exudes a disinterest about her influence while Mason lives in increasing doubt about his own.

Linklater develops Mason's perspective on his mother through three scenes over the subsequent evening. In an echo of the opening shot, we see Mason lounging on a large stuffed animal with his arms behind his head, except this time he is mindlessly watching television when Olivia's boyfriend Ted (Steven Prince) shows up.[7] In what becomes a strategic point-of-audition shot, Mason listens to Ted express contempt that Olivia could not find a babysitter so that the two of them could go out for the evening. This inadvertent eavesdropping will also repeat itself in Mason's further initial observations of Olivia's beaus, as he becomes more concerned with the outcomes of her relationships. Olivia explains to Ted that she has an obligation to stay home with her kids that evening, which Linklater immediately thereafter demonstrates with her reading *Harry Potter and the Chamber of Secrets* to the two of them, cuddled up with her in bed. (The 1998 book was adapted into a feature film that year.) This will be the single moment in the film when we see all three of them in the same intimate space, as the children's comfort with maternal closeness later gives way to the distance that arrives with independence. (See Figure 3.1.)

Figure 3.1 Olivia reads to Sam and Mason all snuggled together in bed

Linklater closes our first day in Mason's life with a poignant scene of the boy being disturbed in his sleep by a heated argument between his mother and Ted, who has returned after going out drinking with his buddies and further berates her about not having more time for him. Mason pursues the sound and spots Olivia hollering one of the most affecting lines of the film: 'I was someone's daughter, then I was somebody's fuckin' mother!' Her exasperated exclamation not only establishes her frustration with the rapid and inexplicable speed of her young life so far, it sets up a crucial theme about aging that is central to the film: our familial and personal roles change as we age, often without our control or even our awareness. In the final sequence of the film, Olivia will revisit this concern in more forceful fashion, when Mason goes off to college and she realizes that her role as a mother has now come to some expiration.

The hostility of the confrontation between Olivia and Ted is worth noting as well, because Mason will be further subject to violence due to her partners, particularly her next husband. Mason himself has a strikingly mild disposition, and resists violence the one time we later see him bullied in middle school, which is in distinct contrast to Olivia's three partners, and more in line with the easygoing nature of his father, whom we have yet to meet. He may well learn from these men to avoid aggression, although curiously, the carryover of conflict extends to the next morning, when Mason is again awoken, this time by Sam singing an annoying song an hour before they are due to get out of bed. What on the surface appears as typical sibling friction – with Sam faking tears when Olivia comes in to scold them – is also a lighthearted indication of Mason's feelings of being disadvantaged. His remaining defense is throwing a pillow at Sam, and he will have no more forceful response later in life when Olivia's husbands harangue him, or when his girlfriend cheats on him.

The first break from a daily chronicle occurs in the next scene, when we see Mason playing with Tommy and ogling scantily clad women in a lingerie catalog. Within the story's reality, this day is likely some time later, since that afternoon Olivia will announce that she has made plans to move them to Houston, closer to her mother, which she apparently had not decided prior to her argument with Ted. Linklater's choice of Mason's play activities – as he moves from gliding on a swing alone to pointing out women's breasts with his friend – is an unusual declaration of sexual interest for the boy, because he otherwise has few expressions of eroticism. In fact, in the two further instances when Mason shows sexual interest, he is also with other boys, and when he begins dating a girl, we never hear him talk about her in sexual terms (although they evidently consummate their relationship). This is one aspect of Mason's development about which Linklater is rather coy, emphasizing the very private nature of his protagonist's sexual practice.

Mason's curiosities about sexuality then turn to contemplations of death, as we see him observing a decomposing bird in the dirt next to his house. This is a fleeting scene, but Linklater (2014, p. 8) has said that it was an archetypal memory from his own childhood, and it certainly makes an implicit statement on Mason's growing realizations of time passing, as the bird's body is beyond death and returning to the earth. Children's discoveries of death, and the truth that life is limited, are a vital part of their maturation process, and Mason's brooding expression silently suggests that he has begun some meditation on his own mortality.

Olivia's later revelation of their impending move will be another form of mortality for Mason, as he realizes that he will no longer have the friends he now enjoys, or the life that he has known. While Sam is more humorously resistant to their mother's decision, Mason continues in a wistful mode as he later lies in bed and sensitively asks Olivia if she still loves his father. She says she does, yet he is less concerned with her feelings about him than their connection to him, as he further asks how his father will find them after they move. At this point, we begin to realize how little Mason knows about what happened between his parents, or even where his father lives (presumably in Alaska), maintaining Linklater's aim of demonstrating the confusion that children have about their parents.[8]

After another ellipsis, supposedly of many days during which Olivia has had time to pack up their belongings, we return to the trio on the last day spent in this home. With striking visual symbolism, Olivia enlists Mason in painting over the murals that adorn the wall next to the bunk bed he shared with Sam, and then asks him to cover the door trim indicating their individual heights over the past many years. Mason is thus engaged in a literal erasure of his past, wiping out proof of the progress he has made during his time in this place, and abandoning a visible history to move on to an uncertain future. The lines marking their increasing stature are etched with dates revealing that this is the house where Mason has done all of his growing up so far, and since he will not live in any other residence for as long, this deletion is more ominous than merely evocative.

Sam meanwhile maintains her detachment, talking on the phone with a friend about their scouting activities, an ephemeral priority that she will never mention again. As if to emphasize this childish fixation on the trivial, Sam then proceeds to whine about the plants and discarded toys they are leaving behind when they finally vacate the house. Again in contrast to his sister, Mason quietly observes his friend Tommy riding on his bike, following after their car and waving goodbye. Mason looks back in tentative reflection, as if slowly realizing this is just another of many departures in his life that he will not control, and Tommy is just another transitory figure who has shaped a short segment of his past yet will be absent from his future.

Similar to the previous shot of Mason observing the dead bird, Linklater includes a short scene that seems to be of little consequence, when Mason and Sam taunt each other in the backseat during the car ride to Houston. Like many supposedly uneventful moments in the film, the playful fisticuffs between the siblings do not advance the narrative but represent a typical experience in Mason's life that he might well remember on such an otherwise momentous day. Linklater will continue to feature such quotidian elements in Mason's evolution, pointing to the often arbitrary nature of our memories. Sam and Mason have apparently fought with each other so much that Olivia has an already established policy of erecting a 'pillow barrier' between them, so this particular activity is nothing new; what matters is the context in which it happens.

The same applies to the final shot in this sequence, with Olivia pulling the car into the parking lot of their new apartment complex. This is their arrival at a new chapter, with the fading sun punctuating the closure of the previous chapter. This is also a shot that Linklater did not place in the script, as he and Adair had planned a different transition to the next scene, advancing into the second year. Rather than the existing cut from the exterior of the apartment building to the interior of Mason's bedroom beginning the next year, they had made the transition with Mason entering the empty apartment in Year One and appearing on the other side of the door in Year Two (Lucca 2015). Such a shift might have been too conspicuous, and Adair claims that working out the more subtle transition of Mason from exterior to interior gave them a better means of making the sutures between years more seamless.

Year two [0:11:20–0:24:48]

Mason is about eight years old in the spring of 2004. The story action takes place on two different days.

1   Olivia tells Mason and Sam over breakfast that Dad (Mason Sr.) will be visiting.
2   Mason works on a computer and Texas mobile at school [later that day].
3   The kids get excited when Dad picks them up at Grandma's house [that afternoon].
4   Dad takes the kids bowling [later that day].
5   Dad talks to them about politics, and they ask if he's coming back [later that day].
6   The kids show Dad their artifacts at home, until Olivia shows up [later that day].
7   Mason goes to a class with Olivia, and sees Bill flirt with her [on a different day].

When Mason next enters the frame in his bedroom of their new apartment, the annual difference is indeed slight. As Olivia yells at him to hurry up for the school bus, we notice that his surroundings have changed, but he appears rather similar, making this one of the most inconspicuous time lapses in the film. Moreover, the last dramatic action of Sam and Mason tussling in the car is somewhat carried over here, as she serves him a pancake while speaking in a deliberately annoying fake language ('I affatay servay yoohay') that she knows will get on his nerves. Sam adds further insult in responding to his complaining by pointing out that Mason 'did officially flunk first grade,' and though no more mention is made of his academic struggles, Sam will later boast of her stellar grades to their grandmother in another tactic to lord over her younger brother.

The more meaningful consequence of this scene is Olivia's announcement to Mason and Sam that their father will be returning to town 'for the day,' to which the kids respond with mild enthusiasm (to avoid confusion, I hereafter refer to Mason Sr. as Dad). Mason's first question gets at his lingering hope – 'Is he moving back?' – though Sam's response is more contemptuous, exaggerating that 'We haven't seen *him* in about 80 years.' In reality, as Olivia points out, his time away has been closer to a year-and-a-half, an absence that we will gradually realize has had more impact on Mason. Sam's defenses remain sarcasm and kvetching, as we saw in the previous relocation scene and will detect during other difficult times; Mason is more ponderous and practical, wondering if he will simply get to see his dad more often.

Later that day we see Mason in a school room; he is playing a game called Oregon Trail on an early twenty-first-century iMac G3 computer, which Linklater said he knew would date that part of the film, since computer designs are so frequent to change.[9] In fact, compared to many children of the era, we see Mason working and playing with media technology relatively little in the film, even as he matures into smartphone use and becomes an avid photographer, a practice that has become increasingly digital in nature over the years. We seldom see Mason engage in any kind of social media, which would become requisite to most adolescent relationships by the end of the 2000s, suggesting how much he is connected to real-life experiences amongst his friends. (This could also be symptomatic of Linklater basing Mason's experiences so much on his own childhood, when youth had no ability to socialize by screen.)

This scene also portends the attention that Mason will enjoy from girls who notice him, as one of his classmates imitates their teacher upbraiding him to get off the computer so he can complete a mobile about Texas. This unnamed girl gives him a smile while he gets to work, and the gesture will be amplified in rather similar terms a few years later when he goes off to school with a drastic haircut. In that scene, after reciting the Texas Pledge, Mason is hailed with a note from a girl across the room who lets him know, again with a smile, that she likes his new look. We will witness further flirtations from girls as Mason moves through other social circles, affections that he rarely invites. So it would seem, at this young age Mason had already adopted the appealing and aloof manner that would draw girls to him.

The day remains more momentous given the arrival of Dad in the next scene. Linklater uses this moment to introduce Catherine (Libby Villari), Olivia's mother and ostensibly a major family figure to Mason and Sam, because they now live much closer to her – although this is only the first of three scenes in which she will appear. Catherine is an encouraging figure to the kids, as she indulges Sam's celebration of her own schoolwork and allows Mason some candy, yet when Dad arrives she clearly stands out against their elation. While the kids gather their bags, Catherine offers thinly veiled suggestions to Dad that he has been irresponsible ('So, Alaska, huh? Are you back?') and that her daughter has taken up his slack ('She's back in school. But she's working and single parenting. A lot to juggle.'). This is an understandable tension, and it is expressed during one of the few moments in the film when Mason is not present. This staging is not a careless choice for Linklater, who otherwise tethers the diegesis to Mason, because as we will become aware when adults later express apprehensions away from Mason, he is nonetheless attuned to their attitudes, as many children are, particularly with family.

This scene also introduces another small yet significant role, that of the '68 GTO that Dad drives.[10] The car is patently indicative of this young father's youthful and unsettled spirit, an imperious muscle car that does not contain seatbelts for his kids – which may add to Mason's thrill at being allowed to ride in the front seat. (See Figure 3.2.) Andrew O'Hehir (2014) sees the GTO as an integral part of Linklater's statement on Dad, who for much of his kids' young lives is 'a semi-employed and unreliable deadbeat with a cool car, who wants to experience all the most fun and dramatic parts of fatherhood without putting in the work.' As we will see, though, in less than a decade Dad exchanges the car to put in the work of fatherhood later in life, and thus we finally verify the elder relinquishing his own boyhood.

Such a statement on youth is then shrewdly countered as the trio moves on to a bowling alley, where Mason is frustrated by the lack of bumpers in the lanes' gutters, and Dad tells him plainly that 'Bumpers are for kids,' a sentiment that he then expands into a half-hearted afterthought in an attempt to embolden the boy: 'Life doesn't give you bumpers.'[11] Linklater will provide further opportunities for Dad to dispense such mild musings throughout the story, although they are never based on any grand philosophy.[12] As we soon come to see, Dad simply wants the best for his kids; his politics

Figure 3.2 Dad shows up to take the kids out in his sporty car

are left of center yet not fueled by any intellectual pretense, and his moral compass is set by pragmatism (even after he later marries a woman from a devoutly Christian family).

Maintaining the theme of Dad giving advice, he becomes more assertive as he and the kids watch TV news at a restaurant within the bowling alley. At this point in history, the so-called Iraq War had begun, with private contractors hired as 'operatives' who became targets in attacks, as the family overhears playing out on screen.[13] Just as Dad goes into a tirade to tell his kids that 'Anybody but Bush!' is a better candidate for president in the upcoming election, they quickly move the conversation to the more pressing matter of his presence in their lives. On this topic, he is far more equivocal and unsure, explaining that he doesn't know if he will move back to the area, and insinuating that Olivia has the option for them to become a couple again, a concept that she never seems to entertain in the entire story.

Linklater connects this line of conversation to a more profound statement on the nature of memory, as Sam recalls how her parents fought so much just a few years earlier. Dad is somewhat saddened and incredulous about her statement, because he recalls happier times ('trips to Galveston, camping in Big Bend, all the fun we had'), not recognizing that his older child was alas affected by what he himself must have considered more tedious disputes with Olivia. Concerns about differences of perceptions and memories from personal experiences will permeate further aspects of the story, demonstrating the contrasting impacts and divergent priorities with which individuals invest their histories.[14] We will encounter moments when Mason reveals the internalized significance of certain memories that his family and friends do not share, which promotes Linklater's suggestion that we all construct our views of life based on rather idiosyncratic perceptions of our experiences:

> Our fundamental view of the world is measured by who we are today and who we've been, and that's not going anywhere. It's only expanding throughout our lives, it's always profound and inescapable how we perceive the world through that viewpoint. So I think this movie conjures something in that area that's really fundamental to how we process the world and time.
>
> (Tobias 2014)

Mason next shifts the conversation to what Dad did in Alaska, trying to elicit adventurous tales of polar bears or other exploits. Dad doesn't have such tales to tell though – he intimates that his time there was much less spectacular – and he becomes more concerned with explaining that he 'just needed to take some time' to get away from the fallout of the divorce. This is a concept that he realizes the kids do not understand, and he stammers in his explanation, much as parents do in relating 'adult' matters to their children. Again, their interest is not in his feelings, but in how he relates to them, as shown clearly in the subsequent scene at Olivia's apartment, when Mason shows Dad his arrowhead collection and Sam displays pictures of her playing basketball.

These few moments of revelry, in which Dad is meagerly trying to catch up on some of the time he has missed with his kids, is then disrupted when Olivia returns home and asks to speak to Dad outside. Linklater does not provide the audio of the ex-couple's conversation, since the kids can tell from their parents' body language that the friction between them is fierce, yet Mason still hints to Sam of his hope that Dad will stay. The camera perspective is critical here, as the kids look down from the second floor, once again isolated from the adult experiences that have driven their parents apart, and are left to infer about the details. They have little outlet for their disappointment, just as they have little explanation for the recurring troubles that cause it.

The editing of the next scene is crucial as well, because Linklater moves away from the family unit to show Olivia taking Mason with her to a college psychology class, and this moment will represent a turning point for the entire family, although its dramatic import initially appears minimal. The professor of the class, whom we will later know as Bill Welbrock (Marco Perella), is coincidentally speaking on the topic of unconditioned responses, and even moves the examples to sexual attraction, heralding the otherwise quite conditioned response he has to the attractive Olivia. After she later introduces Bill to Mason, the teacher tries to ingratiate himself by referring to his own son of a similar age, and then wastes no further time in coming on to his adult student. Welbrock is thus portrayed in somewhat unsavory tones, as he violates educational decorum and – while Mason watches with trepidation – makes a play for the boy's mother. Mason's gaze upon the scene yet again foregrounds his role as an observer of the adult world that is encroaching on him, yet which he can do little to affect. We will see this exchange play out again later in the film when Olivia meets her third husband who, inverting her role with Bill, will be her younger student.

Year three [0:24:49–0:31:42]

Mason is about nine years old in July 2005. The story action takes place over many days.

1 Olivia and Bill return from their honeymoon to their four combined kids.
2 The new family goes out to a nice dinner [likely that night].
3 The stepsiblings walk home with other kids [on a different day].
4 Mason plays video games with stepbrother Randy [later that day].
5 The family plays charades [later that day].
6 The stepsiblings go to a *Harry Potter* book release party [likely a different night].
7 Bill advises his boys on putting, then curses at his own shot [on a different day].
8 Bill leaves the boys in the car to get booze [later that day].

Unlike the previous transition between years, through which we had been prepared for Mason's change of residence, the edit to the next year depicts far more alienating adjustments, as Mason is jostled on a trampoline with Sam and two children, a boy and girl close to their own ages, whom we have not previously seen. An assumption on first viewing could be that these children are merely friends, until we are ourselves jostled by learning that Olivia and Bill are, in fact, returning from a honeymoon to his rather spacious home, and the new kids are now stepsiblings to Mason and Sam. In a more subtle transition, Olivia's children now refer to Bill as 'Dad,' and Bill refers to Olivia's mother Catherine as 'Mom,' as if the apparently short duration of the new couple's marriage has rather immediately yielded an altogether freshly coherent family.

Such harmonious elation soon begins to erode, as we next assess the six members of this new family dining at a fancy restaurant that evening. We learn the names of Mason and Sam's new siblings – Mindy (Jamie Howard) and Randy (Andrew Villarreal) – and they too have assimilated to the practice of referring to Olivia as 'Mom,' yet soon after relating a few moments of their honeymoon in Paris, Bill turns to scolding Randy for playing with an electronic toy at the table and goes on to chastise him for not finishing a school project while they were away.[15] Further, he tellingly orders a second bottle of wine, even though the meal is over and he and Olivia have already finished one bottle together. Not only is Bill controlling in terms of his kids, he's already revealing the encroaching alcoholism that will demean his whole family.

This foreboding tone is suspended during the next few scenes, as first Mason and Sam accompany Mindy and Randy with some neighborhood kids on a walk home from school. In this third year of the story, Mason and Sam are already living in their third residence and apparently attending their third different school, setting up a pattern of instability that will continue until their teens. Bill may seem to hold some promise of consistency given these upheavals and the lack of their father's presence, yet the polished suburban environs and portrait of family cohesion that he promotes are specious.

Linklater then provides an oddly discordant character that momentarily signals some contempt among the kids, when a mentally challenged and older boy named Paul (Ryan Power) walks by the group. An unnamed friend yells to Paul to 'tell us a joke,' to which he responds with a series of curse words. This at once appears to be another random and insignificant moment in Mason's daily experience, yet its incongruous inclusion rises to the level of symbolism, since Paul is not one of these temporarily privileged children, and they are exploiting his affliction for their amusement. Paul is also walking in the opposite direction, so he must not attend the same school, which reinforces his lack of inclusion. Mason has little reaction to Paul's litany of vulgarity, showing his disinterest in participating in the taunting, a character trait that becomes more evident in his future contacts with peers.

The next scenes otherwise continue with examples of Mason's supposedly comfortable new life: he plays a competitive video game at home with Randy, and then plays charades with the entire family, during which Bill shows off his further authority by declaring that no one can use props. This playful mood continues into the next scene, which is one of the few in the film that actually indicates a recorded date: July 15, 2005. The occasion is the book release of *Harry Potter and the Half-Blood Prince* at a local bookstore, complete with children dressed as characters and a countdown until the midnight distribution of the presold copies. (See Figure 3.3.) While Sam appears elated to participate in a trivia contest and receive her book, Lorelei Linklater would later reveal that shooting this scene in costume as Professor McGonagall made her seriously contemplate dropping out of the

Figure 3.3 Mason (in *Harry Potter* glasses) attends a book party with Sam and his stepsiblings Randy and Mindy

production. Linklater explained that his daughter took the books quite seriously ('She thought she might date Harry Potter' [Gritten 2015]) and the younger Linklater – then eleven years old – was so uncomfortable with what she perceived as a violation of this sacrosanct canon that she asked her father to kill off her Sam character (Bibbiani 2014).

As previously noted, the parallel development of the *Harry Potter* series during the production of *Boyhood* was apparent to the young cast members who were reading the books and seeing the films, but also to Linklater himself, who knew that the boy wizard was essentially growing up alongside his own protagonist. Given that *Harry Potter* is one of the very few pop culture phenomena that Mason is shown to enjoy in the film (we are otherwise given little sense for his taste in music, movies, or television), Linklater imbues the books with a conscious recognition. As we will later learn, Mason does indeed wonder about magic in the world, yet will discover through his experiences that life itself holds milder mysteries.

Play continues as a theme in the next scene, in which Bill has taken Mason and Randy to a golf course. Once again the simmering anger within Bill is easily detectable as he continues to criticize Randy, in this case about his golf swing. Parents in mixed families may have any number of reasons for being harder on their own children than their stepchildren – perhaps having less patience with them because they diagnose their own shortcomings through their offspring – but Bill's continuing contempt toward Randy while praising Mason remains discomfiting. In fact, Bill's *self*-contempt is confirmed when he next addresses a ball in what he calls a 'birdie putt,' then promptly misses the shot. Rather than taking the gaffe in stride as part of their lighthearted practice, Bill swears and strikes the green with his club, causing a divot that he sloppily pounds back down and promptly walks away from.

Bill seems to be in competition with himself in this case, and he carries that conflict further a few minutes later when he stops at a local liquor store and leaves the boys to wait in the car. He mentions to them that he is only stopping 'in case we have guests this weekend,' but Randy is smart to his motives, as he tells Mason, 'He always says that, but we never have guests.' Randy's intuition about his father's drinking may explain some of the hostility Bill shows toward him, and with the next scene Linklater shows Bill further indulging his alcoholic excesses.

Year four [0:31:43–0:49:23]

Mason is about ten years old in April 2006. The story action takes place over two or more different days.

1   Bill hides his drinking and scolds the kids, then Dad picks up Mason and Sam.
2   Dad appeals to his kids to talk about their lives [later that day].
3   The three identify butterflies in a lepidopterarium [later that day].
4   The three play hide-and-seek and toss a football in a park [later that day].
5   Mason asks Dad about his employment during an Astros game [that evening].
6   Dad brings Mason and Sam back to his apartment and sings a song [that night].
7   Dad checks on Sam going to sleep [later that night].
8   Dad answers some of Mason's questions about magic [later that night].
9   Dad drops off Mason and Sam at home [the next morning].
10 Mason and Randy find internet porn with a friend [later that day].
11 Bill takes Mason to get his long hair cut off [later that day].
12 Mason fakes being sick in an effort to avoid going to school [the next day].
13 Olivia takes Mason to school late and a girl gives him a nice note [later that day].

The connecting edit that occurs next is one of the most logical in the film, as we see Bill pouring a large amount of vodka (with a slight splash of soda) into a cup, and then surreptitiously hiding the bottle behind laundry detergents in a cupboard. Yet the logic that has us connect this drink to the liquor store visit in the previous scene is deceptive, because we soon realize that Linklater has advanced the story by another year, a year in which Bill's behavior has apparently escalated to the point that he has taken to hiding his drinking rather than merely lying about it.

The first visible indication of the time lapse is then noticeable when Sam is revealed to have much longer hair, and in similar fashion, we will soon see Mason with longer hair than ever before. The kids are not only older, but occupied with more adult tasks, specifically, chores that Bill has assigned them to do while he enjoys walking around the house with his drink in hand. As Sam and Mindy tend to dishes in the kitchen, Bill reminds them of additional work (such as dusting), which he is disappointed to learn Sam has not completed, despite a 'little art project' she finished earlier. Clearly anything she might enjoy creatively is of less interest to him than the work he wants done.

Bill's tyrannical attitude then persists in his reprimand of Mason and Randy, who have been in the back yard pulling weeds but whose work he estimates is just half done. His antagonism may be in advance of a visit from Mason and Sam's father, who has just arrived; the stepfather may want to have another opportunity to exert authority. Yet Bill is not finished with his grousing, which he next turns upon Olivia, whom he enlists to join him in enforcing the expectation that the kids' chores will be completed the next day when they return. This leveraging goes further when Bill next addresses Sam in the third person, telling Olivia, 'Don't let her back-talk me in front of the other kids, please.' The scene could be just an innocuous example of kids resisting toil, yet Linklater uses it to suggest the compromises that Olivia has made through her marriage, because her studying is disrupted by Bill's need for attention, and he is manipulating her to take sides against *her* children. In a subtle suggestion of Bill's lingering toxicity, Linklater continues the scene for a moment after Mason has exited (one of the few times in the film he does so), with Bill intimating to Olivia that she needs to be stricter, which is a further denigration of her maternal skills. Even with the children gone, Bill maintains a captive audience for his derision.

In dramatic disparity, Mason and Sam depart from Bill's lovely house of rules to join their prodigal father, who carries them away in the old GTO that connotes his lawless spirit. Dad also shows that he is more attentive to their lives, as he quickly senses their reticence to talk about themselves. Dad expresses interest in Sam's sculpture project, but then when she claims that it's about 'nothing,' he launches into a monologue to explain to his kids the importance of their communication, setting up an unveiled comparison to Bill:

No, that is not how we are going to talk to one another. All right? No, I will not be that guy. You cannot put me in that category, all right? 'The biological father that I spend every other week with, and I make polite conversation, you know, while he drives me places and buys me shit.' No! Talk to me.

Dad goes so far as to imitate how Mason and Sam might talk to him, about their friends or about their schoolwork, eliciting their bemused response. Mason's rejoinder catches Dad off-guard, though, because he asks his father to talk about his own life as well, giving him pause. Dad thus realizes that he is actually trying *too* hard, and resolves to 'just let it happen more natural,' which is a quality that, despite their times apart, the three of them clearly share in much more discernable ways than the kids do with their stepfather.

Linklater then proceeds to celebrate that inherent familiarity among them, as the trio heads into Houston and stops at a butterfly conservatory, then plays hide-and-seek and tosses a football in a city park. These scenes of Dad being 'natural' with his children are further contrast to their oppressive home life, and in another point of comparison, Dad casually coaches Mason on the basic points of catching a football, quite unlike the tensely refined golf lesson he previously endured with Bill. Such 'teachable moments' are actually a trait of Linklater's movies, which Seth Stevenson (2014) identifies throughout his oeuvre, arguing that the auteur 'has made it his project to chronicle the ways in which we mold and, in turn, are molded by the other people who float through our lives.' We certainly witness this throughout *Boyhood*, more often with Mason outside of formal schooling, and rather in woods and fields, or at bowling alleys and parties.

Continuing with a sports theme, we next see Roger Clemens on the mound pitching for the Houston Astros against the Milwaukee Brewers.[16] Dad expresses his admiration for the aging star's pitching prowess, and these comments on his proficiency seem to motivate Mason to ask his father if *he* has a job.[17] Dad reacts with surprise, and Mason admits that Olivia prompted the question, to which Dad replies with a cocky swagger, stating that he has passed his second actuarial exam, presumably en route to a career in the insurance business. Just as Linklater's parents divorced when he was young and his mother went back to college, his father became an insurance officer, and this choice of profession for the father is not merely autobiographical, but a more telling indicator of how Dad is becoming more grounded and reliable himself (Dawidoff 2015).

At the end of this eventful day, Dad brings Mason and Sam back to his apartment, which refutes his more mature ambitions when he discovers his roommate Jimmy (Charlie Sexton) watching a horror movie with dirty dishes and marijuana paraphernalia spread across a coffee table. Dad chides Jimmy, but their easy banter – and the relaxed manner in which Mason and Sam flop onto the furniture – reveals that even this embarrassment does not rise to the level of offense the kids encountered by not doing all their chores.

A short time later, Ethan Hawke sings 'Split the Difference' while playing an electronic keyboard, the first of two songs that the actor specially wrote for the film. As Dad sings it to his kids with Jimmy playing guitar, the highly specific lyrics speak to their current circumstances, referring to their home in Houston and their mother's new husband. More critically, through this 'lullaby' Dad expresses his frustration in missing them, and ponders how much they have missed him. This is another of the many songs in the film with literal connections to the characters. The lines not only uncover an affective depth to the father's feelings (he has indeed continued writing songs as he claimed he did in Alaska when he was away), but also provide some telling narrative background to events that we do not see, such as Mason painting 'pictures of a family all in blue' and 'whispering to the window, "Will Daddy please come home?"' If Dad is purely fabricating these scenes, they are still sympathetic to Mason's experiences and emotions, with insight to his son's life without him.

The subsequent scenes are intriguing too. They both portray bedtime rituals: Dad checks on Sam, who has gone to bed in what seems to be her father's room, and later he and Mason talk on adjoining couches as they read before sleeping. The exchange with Sam feels uneventful, although it is notable for not featuring Mason, except by name, when she jokes to her father that she's sorry Mason was part of their 'fun day.' Sam will make other sporadic references to her brother being a bother, yet overall their sibling tension is relatively mild. Sam never seems to dislike Mason so much as she wants to emphasize that she is somehow smarter and cooler.

The latter scene is more compelling, as Mason opens with the portentous question to his father, 'There's no like . . . real magic in the world, right?' The metaphysical nature of the question at first sounds enormous, but he goes on to qualify it, apropos of his *Harry Potter* hobby, 'You know, like elves and stuff.' Dad is not dismissive, and instead expands upon Mason's proposition, using a whale as an example of something that otherwise seems rather magical . . . until Mason returns to the more specific point, which is that there are no elves in the world. 'No,' his father responds, 'Technically, no elves.' The humor in this clarification arises not from Mason's calm acceptance, but in Dad's matter-of-fact declaration that, notwithstanding the magical nature of whales, there basically are no elves, which gives Mason some firmer grounding in his own perspective on magic. What seems like another inane conversation is principally indicative of a further stage in Mason's development toward adulthood, as he is leaving the childish imagination that permits elves and begins confronting more banal realities.

Figure 3.4 Mason is incensed about the haircut his stepfather Bill demands

The next day, Dad drops his kids back at their new home, whereupon Link-later begins one of the most visible transformations of Mason in the film, a dramatic haircut that Bill insists on (see Figure 3.4). Given the events of the previous day – and that Mason and Randy are scanning pictures of internet porn with another friend when Bill calls for them – the forceful nature of the haircut can easily be read as a punitive response from the stepfather. At the same time, it operates on other levels as well: Bill is giving Mason a physical demonstration of his dominion over him, and in attempting to make him 'look like a man instead of like a little girl,' Bill is adding a masculinist dimension to this sense of power, which he will soon use against his own wife as well.

Themes of Mason's physical transformation are, of course, germane to the rest of the film, as we watch him change in numerous ways across time, only the immediacy and shock of this haircut challenge the typical subtlety of his bodily evolution. Linklater had in reality directed Coltrane to let his hair grow during the months before, so that this scene would have more visual impact, which was one of the few advance strategies for physical changes the director worked into the story.[18] Further changes in hairstyle (and at the very end, facial hair) will be noticeable, but seemingly motivated by Mason's own predilections, so within the story this traumatic experience gives him a fundamental inspiration to regulate his own image thereafter.

That motivation begins to brew the next morning when Mason fakes being sick to avoid going to school with his newly shorn head. His siblings tease him, but Olivia pursues the matter, driving Mason to school and giving him a chance to express, for the first time in the story, some of his real feelings about Bill. Olivia understands why he is angry about the imposed haircut, until Mason makes a powerful proclamation as a question: 'Why'd you even marry him? He's such a jerk.' Bill has certainly earned this denunciation, while Mason's resentment is more crucially directed at his mother, who tries to rationalize her decision by damning her husband with faint praise: 'Bill has his good qualities. . . . And now we have a family.' Given that the film is all but exclusively built around Mason's perspective, we understandably wonder, along with him, why she would settle for this 'jerk' to somehow form a family, à la *The Brady Bunch* from 1970s television. As Mason retorts, 'We already had a family,' a sensitive statement on the needs he sees fulfilled by his mother and sister, and making an inherent reference to his absent father. This will be one of the few times in the film when Mason actually shows anger toward either of his parents.

Linklater then closes this sequence with a slight redemption for his protagonist, who sulks into class and tolerates some gasps and giggles from his classmates who immediately notice his lack of hair.[19] As the teacher proceeds with a lesson on mythological gods and monsters, Mason is relieved by a far more earthly communiqué from a girl named Nicole (Marina Arellano), who sends a note across the room to tell him, 'I think your hair looks kewl!' Once again he has drawn the attention of a flirtatious girl, who not only senses his inner irritation, but her own opportunity to ease it, which foretells the relationship he will have with his long-term girlfriend in high school, and connects to the new girl he will meet in the last scenes of the film.

Year five [0:49:24–1:01:20]

Mason is about eleven years old in 2007. The story action takes place over three or more different days.

1 Mason and Randy return home to find Olivia crying on the floor of the garage.
2 Bill erupts in drunken violence over dinner [later that day].
3 The siblings talk about Bill's drinking behavior [that night].
4 Bill questions the kids about Olivia's whereabouts [could be the next day].
5 Bill goes to a liquor store and scares the kids while driving drunk [later that day].
6 Olivia shows up with her friend Carol to get Mason and Sam [later that day].
7 Mason plays video games as Olivia cries over their situation [later that day].
8 Sam complains to Olivia before going to a new school [the next day].
9 Olivia walks Mason to class at another new school [later that day].

The edit into this next year is one of the more conspicuous in the film, as we next see Mason with a full head of hair, riding his bike with Randy. As Olivia had reassured him in the previous scene, his hair did indeed grow back, and he appears quite happy riding along with his stepbrother and a skateboarding friend.

This casual moment of revelry is soon disturbed when Mason and Randy ride up to their house and find Olivia crying, stretched out on the floor of the garage. They immediately express their concern for her, yet she tells them to go into the house, whereupon Bill appears, insisting that 'your mother had a little accident.' Even more telling than Bill's violent shouting (ordering Olivia to 'get off the fucking floor') is Linklater's timing and framing of the scene. Olivia's position on the floor and overt shame attest that this was no accident, while the boys are left to envision the violence that had previously taken place. Further, the camera remains outside the half-closed garage door, so that we do not see Bill's face, and so that this domestic disturbance further remains out of view. The use of ambiguity and subject position here is notable, enlisting the audience in further constructing Bill's brutality and suggesting how his children are vulnerable to it as well.

The menacing tone continues directly into the next scene, as a short time later the family is eating dinner when Bill arrives to the table carrying an almost empty bottle of bourbon. With his alcoholism clearly exposed and unabated, he challenges everyone at the table to disagree with his further drinking, and the children are all but paralyzed with fear. Because he is looking for the easiest target to attack, he chooses Mason to act against, throwing a glass that shatters in front of him. This outburst is not enough, though, and Bill then flings his liquor bottle onto the floor next to Randy, barking at him to clean it up. As Olivia screams in desperation and the kids remain transfixed in silence, Bill hurls plates onto the floor and towers over his prey until he turns to walk away.

This scene is perhaps the most dramatic, and certainly the most vicious, in the film. Linklater has smartly given us little reason to explain Bill's reprehensible behavior, because its etiology is essentially irrelevant to those it affects the deepest, his family. They simply see a man out of control, desperate for attention, and truculent in his actions. For children, motives for parental behavior are rarely considered, as they are far more invested in the manifest emotions evinced by their actions. In Bill's case, we have never seen him as very loving to begin with, and his previously indirect antagonisms have really become more callous over time, leading to this inevitable outburst.

Understandably, Mason and the other kids do not know what to make of the whole situation, and that night they gather in a bedroom to discuss their father. At the moment, Mason is sublimating his discomfort with a laptop computer on which he is watching a humorous YouTube sketch from 2007 known as *The Landlord*, wherein a toddler demands money from a tenant – and counter to his current situation, the child becomes violent and drinks alcohol.[20] This diversion offers distinctly mordant contrast in providing Mason with a comical outlet for the anxiety the rest of his siblings are expressing about Bill, but they clearly do not know how to manage the crisis. As if provoked when the toddler in the video brings up her own drinking ('I need to get my drink on – can I have four beers?'), Mason turns to his stepsiblings and asks if Bill has 'ever gotten this bad before,' seeking some standard of comparison, to which Randy and Mindy respond that Bill is indeed at a new level of agitation.

Technological influence continues into the next scene, likely the following day, when Bill gathers all of the kids in the living room and demands their cell phones. Children in American culture were typically carrying the devices by this point, which gave them a certain level of independent communication that parents could nonetheless exploit, as Bill does by going through their call menus to detect if the missing Olivia has contacted any of them. Curiously, after inspecting Randy's and Mason's phones, he tosses Mindy's back to her and expresses his trust, only to find evidence on Sam's phone that her mother had called. He is incredulous when Sam explains that Olivia left a message stating that she would return later and the kids should stay in their rooms, which prompts Bill to order all of them out to the car.

While we have not seen him drinking at this time, his destination with the kids indicates his thinking, as he drives them to the liquor store. Adding to the shame his kids must feel for his actions, he first orders Mindy to use an ATM machine in front of the store, whereupon he learns that Olivia has emptied their account. This does not prevent him from sloppily writing a check – confirming his inebriation – which he tells Randy and Mason to take in to the store clerk to cash.

The boys' exchange with the clerk is tinged with pathos, as they must present the barely legible check and then point out their dad outside, who cowardly waves from the car. As if by intuition, Randy knows to invent an excuse, that their father isn't 'feeling well,' which is ironically true. Greater irony imbues the clerk's advice to the boys: 'Take care of your dad now, son. You only got the one.' That may be true of Randy, but Bill will be the second of three men Mason sees married to his mother, and his experiences with this stepfather will raise his concerns about Olivia's marriage to the next one. And, of course, these children should not be charged with caring for their parents, particularly when they cannot care for themselves.

In a more terrorizing affront to the children, Bill drives off recklessly with the kids in the car, who scream as he dodges traffic. Linklater may have intended this as the last level of danger that Bill would cross, because the next shot a short time later reveals Olivia showing up to the house to pick up Mason and Sam. The escalating drama of this sequence reaches a closure here, as Olivia calls out for her children and rebukes the belligerent Bill, who appears mildly surprised that she is decisively leaving him. The confrontation between the couple threatens to become violent, despite Olivia bringing her friend Carol (Barbara Chisholm) to literally stand behind her (see Figure 3.5). In fact, Olivia becomes more aggressive in her response to rescuing her kids, screaming at Bill to not touch them after he attempts to block their exit. With Mason and Sam safely escorted to the car by Carol, Olivia maintains her concern for them once she takes the driver's seat, yelling for them to put on their seatbelts (echoing the call of her mother when they previously rode in Dad's car).

Linklater films the departure from Bill's house similar to the family's departure from their home in Year One: Mason and Sam both look back at where they once lived, and wonder where they are going next. Even as Olivia explains that they will be staying with Carol for some time, the siblings realize that they are leaving their third home in five years, as well as the friends (and in this case, family) that they knew there. They have known little of stability.

Figure 3.5 Mason looks in bewilderment at his stepsiblings as Olivia (behind him) pulls him away from their life with Bill

Mason may show resilient recovery from this latest trauma, as we next see him playing a Wii video game at Carol's house with her son Lee (Matthew Martinez-Arndt), yet the nature of the game is not trivial: the boys are literally punching the air as they 'box' with a figure on screen, providing a physical outlet for Mason's latent tension. Samantha is otherwise more expressive in asking her mother about the aftermath, wondering why they left Randy and Mindy behind. As Olivia explains the practical matter – she is not their legal guardian, and she has called Child Protective Services – Sam is rightly concerned for their safety and the possibility that she may never see them again. Ever the older sibling, Sam often points out the perceived injustice that she bears, whereas Mason observes and adapts. Olivia, meanwhile, momentarily breaks down in tears, at a loss for what they will do: 'I don't have the answer to everything.' Emotive scenes like this were no doubt a factor in Academy voters honoring Arquette with a Best Supporting Actress Oscar.

Sam persists with her griping the next morning when Olivia drops her off at a new middle school, enumerating the further annoyances of her current condition: she doesn't know anyone here, she has left her friends and did not say goodbye, she's wearing dirty clothes, and they have no place to live. Olivia explains that she has nonetheless arranged everything for Sam with the school office, but, of course, that is beside the point, because the mayhem of their lives has impacted her on these many other levels. Akin to when they left their house before, Olivia finds herself on the defensive against her daughter, repeating a familiar refrain about Sam's 'horseshit attitude,' and agreeing that this situation 'sucks,' but not 'half as much as having a drunk fool slam your head against a wall!' This is the first and only time in the story that Olivia actually refers to the abuse that Bill inflicted on her, yet the kids do not react, since they already know what happened. And at the height of her shouting, Olivia repeats the now mildly humorous command to Mason to put on his seat belt.

Mason braves his transition to yet another school with more composure, and Olivia walks him to his new class. In a certain demonstration of his burgeoning masculine pride, Mason backs away when she attempts to kiss him, and he proceeds into the classroom to quietly take a seat at the back. His teacher introduces herself, but we quickly sense the more important camaraderie he shares with a new classmate, Kenny (Cambell Westmoreland), who holds out his hand for a slap and coolly intones, 'Welcome to the suck.' (This is military slang used when introducing new soldiers to tough conditions, so Linklater deliberately parallels the 'trenches' of school to those of war.) Before the scene closes, Linklater includes another telling exchange, as the teacher introduces Mason to the class, and we see the close-up blank faces of three classmates staring back at him. Mason yet again finds himself on the outside and quietly trying to fit in, unsure of his place with his peers, a feeling that will recur in his further relationships.

Notes

1 Many of these cases, and a trove of data, can be found in Finley (2014).
2 A recent view of youth as more empowered by technology can be found within most essays of the collection by Kiuchi and Villarruel (2016).
3 In the Criterion DVD (2016a) commentary, Linklater suggests that he had begun with the idea of 'theoretically' making a 120-minute film of twelve ten-minute sections, but after he had so much valuable footage from the first year alone, he realized he wanted to be more flexible with his timing.
4 A banner in the background indicates the month is May, but Linklater (2017) confirmed that he faked the date: 'Even though the first scene implies "May" it was actually later summer 2002 that production began.'
5 Linklater explains that he wanted the songs in the film to have an emotional resonance not only to the scenes but also to the context of the times depicted in the story. See Rothman (2014).
6 Linklater applied some decidedly specific autobiographical quirks to Mason's character. His mother, Diane, reflected on this particular scene from her son's childhood: 'The teacher told me Rick would just sit there and stare outside. So I said, "Rick, Mrs. Arnold said you were just looking out the window all day. What were you doing?" And he said, "I was thinking about playing."' See Nunez (2015).
7 Linklater points out in the Criterion DVD (2016a) commentary that he knew his choices of on-screen media would 'age interestingly' based on their period; in this case, Mason is watching the *Dragon Ball Z* television series (1996–2003).
8 Linklater explains that as a child of divorce, 'you don't really know why your parents broke up. Maybe you overheard a little conflict or a fight, but it'll be a mystery to you your whole life. You won't ever fully know.' See Adams (2014).
9 In terms of aspects that will date the film, Linklater said, 'Technology ultimately is the thing that will change the most in this age. That's the demarcation of these years. Technology, and maybe the haircuts, too.' See Travers (2014).
10 The '68 GTO, and indeed *all* of the cars in the film, are identified on the Internet Movie Cars Database: www.imcdb.org/movie_1065073-Boyhood.html.
11 Bowling was also part of Linklater's childhood experience with his father; see Dawidoff (2015).
12 Sam makes a gesture in this scene that some viewers have interpreted as a marijuana reference to Dad, but her expression suggests that she is reacting more to his odor, as indicated in the script: 'Samantha mimes smoking, points to Dad, as if to say that he smells of cigarettes.' We then see him smoking shortly thereafter.
13 While Linklater shot all the scenes with actors each year as they occurred, he was not averse to some manipulation in postproduction, such as inserting the televised news story in this scene, which he mentions in the Criterion DVD (2016a) commentary. I asked him about this footage because the featured events occurred in late March of 2004, not in 2003 when I assumed the scene was set. Linklater (2017) explained that there had actually been a long lapse 'that turned out to be our largest gap between shooting, [years] 1 and 2, for various reasons: Patricia [Arquette] had a baby and was now on a demanding TV show, I was super busy in post on *School of Rock* and shooting *Before Sunset* in Paris (as was Ethan, who went straight from Paris to another production), and Ellar hadn't grown much at all. The extra year proved advantageous all around. I think the

three of us all felt a little responsible for the scheduling difficulty, and it seemed everyone really doubled down on their commitment to the film and making it work from then on, no matter how busy everyone's schedules.'

14 Linklater far more aggressively depicts competing perceptions of personal memories in *Tape* (2001), a literal one-room real-time drama in which three college friends confront each other about a disputable incident from their past.

15 The toy is a Tamagotchi, a 'virtual pet' developed in Japan during the late 1990s before creating an international sensation in 2005, the year this scene is set. The fad faded in the U.S. within a few years, so this is another moment marked by technological pop culture.

16 Linklater again employed some judicious editing in creating this scene, because Roger Clemens never pitched a game in Houston where Jason Lane homered to left. The footage of Clemens, as confirmed by the background stats on scoreboards, was shot on August 30, 2006. These images had to be cut together with footage of the cast watching the game when Lane did homer to left, which occurred on April 17, 2006. The closer shots of Lane circling the bases may have been edited from another game altogether.

17 Clemens was suspected of achieving his superior pitching late in life through nefarious means but, as Chris Vognar (2014) points out, this 'scene wasn't some kind of in-joke when it was shot; the allegations about performance-enhancing drugs hadn't yet surfaced. Only time could tell. (Well, maybe some of us assumed it back then.)'

18 Coltrane claims his long hair 'was one of the only times they asked me to alter my appearance,' and said he was actually relieved to have it cut off for this scene. See Meyer (2014).

19 Linklater was following recent Texas educational law after S.B. 83 was passed by the Texas legislature in 2003, which made the recitation of the 'Texas Pledge' a requirement at public schools each morning.

20 *The Landlord* can be viewed in various forms on YouTube, including this version with commentary by star Will Farrell: www.youtube.com/watch?v=L4d2nlsoB3.

4 Understanding *Boyhood*

The teenager becomes a man

And so my advice to all young people who wish to become poets is: do
something easy, like learning how to blow up the world – unless you're not
only willing, but glad, to feel and work and fight till you die.

– e. e. cummings (1955)

The progression into adolescence from childhood is fraught with persistent
trepidations for all youth. Expectations rise for young people, as they are
treated by adults with less tolerance and loaded with more responsibilities:
the adolescent needs to attend to social concerns, become more proactive
in self-care, and begin fulfilling goals beyond the protocols of familial and
academic systems. The carefree discoveries of childhood slowly turn into
a cringing realization that one's actions carry consequences beyond home,
and after the internet, beyond school and even community. Meanwhile, the
adolescent mind and body are suffering hormonal surges, resulting in sometimes awkward anatomical growth and an abundance of sexual sensations
that are generally reviled by adult authority. As if those impulses weren't
confusing enough, adolescents stake out identities beyond their treatment
as the children of parents and the students of teachers, leading to perceived
rebellions that are generally just efforts at individuality.

Mason encounters all of these aspects in his ascent to adolescence and
the adulthood waiting beyond. Unlike the protagonists of most teen movies,
however, he does not encounter singular events that define his youth, nor
does he typically exhibit the extreme emotions of so many teenagers that
make for easy comedy or drama. Mason remains a creative iconoclast and
an ambivalent explorer, ever questioning his perceptions of the world while
renouncing his concerns about the world's perception of him. And as he
enters his teenage years, like every adolescent, he is still directed by adult
authority during his efforts to gradually take on the autonomy that will liber-
ate him from the comforts and confines of childhood.

Year six [1:01:21–1:12:09]

Mason has turned thirteen by late 2008. The story action takes place over two consecutive days.

1 Mason and Sam put up Obama election posters on lawns with Dad.
2 Mason and Sam endure Dad's awkward talk about sex [later that day].
3 Dad explains a song to Mason as they drive [later that day].
4 Dad talks about his new career, then swims in a lake with Mason [later that day].
5 Mason and Dad walk through the woods and talk about girlfriends [later that day].
6 Mason and Dad talk over a fire roasting marshmallows [that evening].
7 Dad sings a song in their tent [later that night].
8 Dad tells Mason to piss out their campfire [the next morning].

The intense scenes from the previous year give way to a calmer set of circumstances the next year, during which we never once see Olivia or where Mason and Sam are now living, and thus the typical obligations of narrative exposition and explanation are further elided. Mason is probably thirteen at this point because Sam is later identified as fifteen, and literal signs suggest that this is late 2008: Dad is canvassing a neighborhood as the kids implant lawn banners for the Democratic presidential campaign. Not only is it election season, but this must have been filmed after early September, by which point Barack Obama had announced Joe Biden as his running mate, and based on a later reference, Republican candidate John McCain had selected Sarah Palin.

Linklater integrates yet another commentary on Texas when Mason knocks on a house door clearly labeled 'No Soliciting,' and is then confronted by the middle-aged owner in the driveway. Disregarding both the notice on the door and the large Confederate flag on the garage, Mason casually asks the man if he can place a sign on his lawn, to which the blunt resident retorts, 'Do I look like a Barack Hussein Obama supporter?' before adding, 'I could shoot you.' Mason is the antithesis of confrontational, yet the white man's rhetoric clearly suggests a level of racial antagonism, which is the single time race is candidly referenced in the film.

As he often does with such contentious moments, Linklater provides a contrast to this tension with Sam meeting an effusive Obama supporter, a young mother who expresses an outright romantic affection for the future president. Texas, so it seems, retains some Democrats, including Dad, who drives by to pick up his kids in his GTO and incites Mason to yank a McCain sign off a nearby lawn. Once again expressing his politics, Dad tells them, 'I'm a patriot, all right? And sometimes in this life, you gotta fight.'

Dad's political zeal harkens back to his bowling alley comments on President Bush from earlier in the story, which he seems primed to repeat when we next encounter him and the kids in the restaurant of yet another bowling alley. The crucial difference in this case is that Dad has suspended any political concerns to focus on the personal, diving right into a series of questions to Sam about a party she plans to attend that evening, rather than accompanying him and Mason on a camping trip (we recall from that previous scene that Sam had disparaged their camping trips from childhood). Dad jovially teases Sam about his suspicions that kids will be drinking, signaling that she is now circulating with an older age group, but this is soon enough dismissed by his focus on a more crucial concern, 'that guy on your Facebook page.'

For the first time with either parent, we witness a discussion of potential romance for one of the children, an awkward and delicate topic to be sure, around which Sam feigns confusion in an effort to circumvent her father's recognition of her nascent dating life. In addition to pointing out the tendency of youth to share their lives on social media more than with their parents, Dad draws out the boy's name – Garrett – and further asks Sam if he is her boyfriend, to which she sheepishly replies, 'Kind of.' Her noncommittal response is likely a reflection of her uncertainty about their relationship, but also an attempt to alleviate her father's concern, which does not diminish. Now Dad does turn the topic back to politics, asking Sam, 'What's the one thing you know about Sarah Palin's seventeen-year-old daughter?' Taking the scandal of the time as an opportunity to invoke patriarchy, Dad thus informs Sam that she will *not* be pregnant when she turns seventeen in two years, going on to remark that merely abstaining from sex is an option, but 'that did not work out very well for your mother and me.'[1]

Dad's comment prompts Mason to begin walking away, since this inherent insult only adds to his kids' palpable discomfort about the sex topic, which does not halt his efforts to pursue this matter that he has apparently never discussed with them. In addition to not wanting to reveal to her father if she has had any sexual experience, Sam – like all children – does not want to think about her own parents as sexual beings. Dad nonetheless persists, moving the focus to contraception rather than discussing any sexual activity per se, until an attractive woman named Tammy (Tamara Jolaine) approaches him. Suddenly, Dad now finds himself in an ironically unnerving position, as Tammy's familiarity with him betrays that they have had their own romantic history, which he thereafter attempts to defuse by returning to his point about pregnancy.

Dad's focus on Sam getting pregnant, as compared to Mason getting a girl pregnant, reveals some sexism on his part. He is understandably concerned about his teenage daughter, and he admonishes her to use contraception, specifically condoms. The suggestion makes Sam squirm, as he timidly adds, 'wear a condom – or get Garrett to, I don't know.' There is clumsy comfort in Dad encouraging his daughter to take authority in protecting herself from pregnancy, although he directs none of this advice to Mason. Granted, the boy may not yet be pursuing sexual activity, but by omitting any mention of Mason's future concern for contraception, and suggesting that Sam should 'get Garrett to' use condoms, Dad exhibits a passive attitude for male liability in sexual matters.

Picking up with the previous reference to Olivia, Dad explains that they were both 23 when they had Sam, leading him to a more poignant confession: 'We didn't put ourselves in the best position to be great parents. And I wish that – I wish I were a better parent to you guys, all right? And I, I hope that you can learn from my mistakes, okay?' Linklater uses this scene as another indicator of the father's growing insight and responsibility, as well as the learning process that he implicitly depicts in action throughout the lives of all the characters. More so than Sam, Mason will question his own judgment and ponder his mistakes, especially in his most serious romance before college. Sam, in the meanwhile, will not be subject to any more parental questioning of her love life in the story, and Garrett, who remains unseen and may not be so significant after all, will never be mentioned again.

The ensuing camping trip with Mason and Dad concludes the film's coverage of this year, starting with a scene inside the GTO as Dad explains the 2007 Wilco song 'Hate It Here' to his captive son. Such moments build the father's musical appreciation (he compares the album to The Beatles' *Abbey Road*), while also displaying his efforts to influence his son's own artistic acumen, as he expounds upon the 'old school' simplicity of the song. We will later be reminded that this is a style Dad embraces in his own songwriting.

Father and son have more bonding opportunities over the course of the day, first setting out to swim in a lake. Linklater shoots their casual disrobing in juxtaposition to the prospective gravity of their discussion, as Mason realizes that the family may be facing yet another relocation since his mother is finishing her master's degree and applying to teaching positions.[2] Dad tries to reassure Mason that he will still come to visit every other weekend, maintaining his consistent presence in Mason's life, adding, 'We'll just roll with it.' Further, Dad reveals that he is now working for an insurance company – his actuarial studies having apparently paid off – but points out that the business is not reliable, and his avocation as a musician is not lucrative. This is a subtle dose of economic precaution for Mason, particularly with the Great Recession setting in that year, because he will later find his own labor value in service rather than creativity.

Their next conversation is more intimate, as Mason asks his dad whether Tammy is his girlfriend. Once again evading his own romantic experience, Dad does not provide a direct answer, other than to admit he has kissed her, and he turns the question back on Mason. Continuing with the tentative candor that he has learned from his sister, Mason responds that he 'sort of' has a girlfriend, whom he has 'not really' kissed. Mason's further comments are also emblematic of adolescent romance, as he elaborates that they seem to have little in common when they talk (she does not share his taste in video games or movies). Dad quickly recognizes his son's frustration and again offers some reasonable advice, telling him to 'actually be interested in her' by asking questions and listening to the answers. As Mason confronts the misgivings and mysteries of young love, his father attempts to instill some confidence in him, not admitting to his own uncertainty. The symbolism of the setting around this conversation is also significant: the camera follows them through thickening brush and trees, which surround them in their expedition to nowhere in particular (see Figure 4.1). Mason will not emerge from these woods in his youth, at least not until he finds himself in the desert in college.

Mason and Dad have another exchange about pop culture that night while making s'mores over a campfire, discussing the possibility of another *Star Wars* movie being made. In reality, a surprisingly unpopular animated film, *The Clone Wars*, had been released as part of the franchise in August of 2008, and plans for a seventh episodic film in the series, *The Force Awakens*, would not be announced for another four years (and that film would

Figure 4.1 Dad gives Mason some advice as they wander through the woods

not appear until a year after *Boyhood*). Thus, Linklater may have intended Mason's skeptical comments about continuing the series as a critical jab after *Clone Wars*, yet the more consequential revelation is their shared generational experience of the preceding two trilogies across the decades of their youth. Deducing from other references, Mason Sr. was born circa 1970 and Mason Jr. circa 1995, and thus the previous films appeared when the father was aged seven to thirteen (1977–1983) and his son was four to ten (1999–2005), marking these sci-fi epics as cultural touchstones of their individual childhoods.

Two short scenes close this year, as we hear just a few lines of Dad singing the song 'L.A. Freeway'[3] later in the tent, and the next morning Mason awakens and pees on the remnants of their smoldering fire, which Dad suggests is a 'Native American custom' to 'give back to the Earth what you take from it.' Once again Linklater draws out a telling contrast between scenes, as Dad sings of urban torment in his song that night and the next day takes heed of his natural surroundings. Mason will also find himself in a cycle between city and country, as he continues to relocate to two new homes, and then college, over the next five years. He will have the opportunity to follow his sister to school in Austin, yet decides on the more rural surroundings of a college in Alpine, forsaking metropolitan escapades to enjoy the tranquility of arid plateaus.

Year seven [1:12:10–1:26:35]

Mason is about fourteen and in eighth grade during November 2009. The story action takes place on two different days.

1   Olivia drops Mason off at his middle school, and he walks to his locker.
2   Mason is confronted by two bullies in the bathroom [later that day].
3   Mason talks to his classmate Jill while walking to Olivia's college [later that day].
4   Mason watches Olivia teaching a psychology class [later that day].
5   Olivia reproaches Sam, then Mason's friend Chase invites him out [later that day].
6   Mason hangs out with boys in a house under construction [that night].
7   Olivia has a party and gets friendly with her student Jim [on another day].

The story picks up a little over a year later in November of 2009, and Mason shows signs of a growth spurt in the interim. Linklater meant for this to be a 'collapsed year' that represented Mason's two-year middle school experience, and he quickly establishes the higher stakes of masculinized behavior among boys during these years (Paramount 2014). In fact, the first day of this episode is filled with indicators of Mason's increased interest in girls and his competition with other boys. The morning begins with a fleeting exchange with his classmate Tony (Jordan Howard), who points out a girl he's interested in, to which Mason glibly responds, 'Good luck with that.' This dismissive and aloof attitude will permeate many of his interactions with boys hereafter, as he not only affects a cool demeanor, but also emphasizes his detachment, which alleviates him of the pugnacious nature common to many boys by this age.

Mason is not free from confrontation, though, as witnessed by the two bullies waiting for him when he next goes to the school bathroom. Even though Mason is taller than both of them, they quickly resort to a typically immature feminizing of him in order to stake out their authority, calling him a 'little bitch' and 'pretty boy' as they bump into him and try to touch his hair. Even though one of the bullies attempts to elevate the sexual degradation of Mason by calling him a 'faggot,' they are patently unaware of the latent homosexual tension they express, as they enact their physical contact with him through violence. Linklater does not overtly question the matter of sexual preference for Mason within the story, although this lavatory skirmish sets up a certain defensiveness about Mason's sexual authority, which will be made more explicit later that day.

Mason's lack of independence is on display again as he waits for Sam to pick him up after school and then resigns to walk away across the town of San Marcos, the first time in two years that we have seen where he lives. This relocation may still be rather recent, as he soon meets up with a classmate named Jill (Evie Thompson), who asks him how he likes the town, making reference to its location halfway between Austin and San Antonio. Mason reveals that Olivia is now teaching at 'the college' (undoubtedly Texas State University, which is in San Marcos but not named at this point), while in more pressing matters Jill dishes on another classmate who 'cut one of her wrists,' and so she's going to visit her in the hospital. Linklater's dialogue here is rather perceptive, as Jill spends some time discussing the other girl's personal style ('dyed black hair and the nose ring') and disregards any thought of motive for her friend's probable suicide attempt, indicating the superficial priorities of adolescence.

In many ways, the scene plays like the famous 'walking and talking' scenes that Linklater had already made his trademark in *Slacker* and the *Before* films. Mason and Jill are at once discussing the trivia of their daily lives (such as what books they are reading) in addition to revealing subtle details about their personalities, as in Mason's indifferent response to Jill's announcement that a girl named LeeAnne has a 'big crush' on him. When Jill pursues this disclosure by asking Mason if he has a girlfriend, he says with predictable nonchalance, 'Not currently,' exuding a certain confidence in addition to his composure. His behavior affirms his scant curiosity about the possibility of any romantic future with LeeAnne, which is of far less consequence for him than it must be for her, marking a conventional imbalance between the sexes at this age.

When Mason at last makes his way to Olivia teaching a class at the college, she is curiously on the subject of ethology, the study of behavior, particularly John Bowlby's attachment theory. As she explains the concept, Linklater's intent is revealed, offering one of the most blatant philosophical statements he advances in the story: 'human survival depends on us falling in love.' Where previously Bill lectured on innate conditional reflexes (in a very similar setting), now a few years later Olivia lectures on more substantial matters of existence and emotion. As she goes on to specify, the love between a mother and her children is the original grounding of this survival cycle, a cycle that we see fully realized throughout the story, with Olivia raising her kids and sending them off to find their own loves. And during this theorizing on the subject of falling in love, Linklater has inserted the peculiar presence of Jim (Brad Hawkins) as a student in her class, who, much like Olivia did with Bill, listens attentively to the teaching of an older person he will later marry. This relationship will also become another cycle of love and survival.

Mason and Olivia thereafter return to the family apartment, which is a little nicer than where they had lived in Houston before she married Bill. Her first order of business is reprimanding Sam for not picking up Mason at school that afternoon, and the older sister defends herself with an excuse that refers to her embarrassment of having a younger brother in middle school. Sam's concern for her status is further marked by her dyed crimson hair and the presence of a girlfriend sitting on the bed next to her, a concern that Olivia sensibly (and psychologically) challenges: 'Do you want to be a self-centered narcissist?' Clearly Mom has elevated her chastising skills beyond the 'horseshit attitude' realm.

Meanwhile, Mason has his own friends to impress, one of whom, Chase (Sinjin Venegas), drops by to invite him out camping that night. In a vivid departure from the back-to-nature excursion Mason took with his father the previous year, this trip will take him to the building site of an empty house, with no adult presence and far more talk of girls. Still a child though, Mason first asks Olivia for permission.

To further emphasize the difference from last year, Linklater cuts to a scene of Mason with Chase, his older brother Charlie (Nick Krause) – a high school senior and the presumptive authority figure – and two other friends: Tony and one of Charlie's (unnamed) classmates. They are hanging around a half-done room in an unfinished home (perhaps a nod by Linklater that these young men are still under construction themselves), and their current occupation is breaking spare boards in a display of their physical prowess. Chase soon raises the stakes by producing a circular saw blade and throwing it into a sheet of drywall, and not to be outdone in this macho exhibition, Mason immediately follows suit. (See Figure 4.2.)

Two more elements of the evening soon come into play: alcohol and sex. Somewhat impressed with Mason, Charlie offers him a beer, which Mason opens and casually sips. Charlie next tests Tony, who declines the beer, leading to a quick correlation of his drinking and his libido, as Charlie retorts, 'If you're too chicken shit to even have a beer, I know for a fact that you have never gotten any pussy.' The awkward assertions that follow provide some of the most explicit evidence in the story that Mason is understandably unsure of his ascent to masculine sexual practice, as first Chase sheepishly claims to have had sex with a local girl who entertained a few other boys at the same time. The statement is met with vocal derision by his peers, who continue to traffic in the vulgar vernacular that young men use to evade their ignorance of women.

While Tony remains the reasonable voice of skepticism, Charlie next puts Mason on the spot, asking him if he 'ever got any.' As cavalier yet tentative as his beer drinking, Mason responds, 'A few times,' with the classic lie that she lives far away ('back in Houston') and thus the guys would not know her. This fib is not merely an effort to evade his virginal shame, but also an indication of his lingering connection to his recent past, which he can conveniently use as a defense against his awkward present. He amplifies this by

Figure 4.2 Mason casts a diffident look at his buddies acting 'mannish'

explaining that he *would* have sex with local girls, but 'none of [them] want to.' Mason clearly wants to compete with these boys, while the sincerity of his lament reveals his latent (and more potent) frustration with attracting romantic attention.

Tony finally has enough of the bravado from the older boys, and asks them why are they are 'hanging out with a bunch of 8th graders on a Friday night?' Charlie's friend reacts to the affront with an assorted barrage of priapic insults ('penis wrinkle,' 'cum gums,' 'dice danglers,' 'fuzz nut'), until Charlie unveils a further challenge, claiming that they have invited 'some whores' to attend their gathering and promptly testing the younger boys as to whether they are 'in' on this arrangement. Yet again Mason feigns insouciance, but the older boys ridicule Tony's lack of enthusiasm, taunting him by saying he is gay. Linklater once more taps into the adolescent fear of difference and isolation through this dialogue, and also exposes some of the typical masculine insecurity about sexual experience and normality through homophobia, suggesting that even the otherwise well-adjusted Mason is still susceptible to these doubts. Charlie soon enough reveals that the impending arrival of girls was a ruse to test the other boys, proving how easily male confidence can be manipulated, and with logical continuity, they return to their preoccupation with breaking boards. Mason has indeed entered the arena of contested masculinity this year, just in time before high school.

Linklater's depiction of this year then concludes with another scene suggesting Mason's budding sexual shrewdness, although the primary action of the sequence focuses on Olivia, who holds a student party at her apartment with her colleague, Prof. Douglas (Angela Rawna). Olivia acts as hostess, tending to her guests with food, until we find Mason in his bedroom chatting with a female college student who, like Jim, we had also seen previously in his mother's classroom. The conversation is not lascivious in any way, excusing how much Mason again exudes self-possession. She compliments him on a colorful large mural he has painted on his wall – echoing the mural he had in his childhood bedroom, in a graffiti form similar to the style he used in first grade – and she spells out the letters it forms: kezjo. 'It doesn't really mean anything,' Mason readily notes, perhaps defending himself against anticipated interpretation.

Seizing another opportunity to comment on Mason's surroundings, the student asks about a picture of him with his dad, but he deftly deflects this interest into asking the woman about his mother as a professor. Throughout the film, Mason expresses essentially no worries about money, yet this question reminds us that he remains slightly concerned about his parents' vocations, and he is relieved when the student cheerily recounts that Olivia is 'super smart and she cares.' Mason seems to seek this external confirmation of what he observed earlier, as Olivia taught with passion and erudition, and his observation of her is then again tested in the subsequent scene, as he watches his mother become enamored with Jim.

The monologue that Jim then delivers over dinner with Olivia and a few other guests is significant not only for its length (the longest story any character tells in the film), but for its symbolic relevance to Mason. At first Jim speaks with excitement in recalling how his Army unit in Iraq entered villages and treated families to music and toys for kids, then becomes more solemn in explaining that later troops were less amicable and consequently suffered casualties. Jim will similarly entertain Olivia and her family at first – he buys Mason a camera the next year – until the 'matter of mutual respect' (which he claims was so important in war) later dissolves with this family over the next few years. Linklater foreshadows that there will indeed be casualties in Jim's relationship with Olivia, and further, Jim's liminal age between Mason and Olivia – still a student, not yet a parent – will remain a vexation. Jim also represents a cautionary tale for Mason, who is not many years from enlistment age himself.

As if Jim's somber story was not disarming enough, later Mason pensively watches his mother chatting alone with him, while some folks from the party quietly sing Pink Floyd's 'Wish You Were Here.' The song provides an ambiguous punctuation to the scene (could it refer to Olivia's own loneliness, or Mason missing his father?), although the clearer visual connection is to the analogous scene six years earlier, when Mason looked on as Olivia began her relationship with Bill. Once again, his expression turns to apprehension as he ruminates on the entrance of a new father figure into his life, one whose presence is initially reassuring and ultimately spiteful. These parallel shots by Linklater suggest the preternatural wisdom of the child in evaluating potential parental partners; in both cases, he does not initially indicate disapproval, even though his tacit skepticism reveals his doubts. Olivia nonetheless marries each man before another year goes by.

Year eight [1:26:36–1:43:15]

Mason turns fifteen and is now in high school by 2010. The story action takes place on three consecutive days of a weekend.

1   Mason comes home late, and Jim wishes him a happy birthday.
2   Dad arrives with his new wife Annie and baby son [the next day].
3   Dad tells Mason he sold his car and gives him a special gift album [later that day].
4   The family arrives at Annie's parents' house [later that day].
5   Mason receives gifts, including a Bible and a shotgun [later that day].
6   Most of them go out shooting targets [later that day].

7   The family sings Dad's song together on the front porch [that night].
8   The family attends a church sermon [the next day].
9   Mason and Sam express curiosity to Dad about his religion [later that day].

Taking another leap in space as well as time, Linklater opens the next year in front of a new house that Mason now calls home, this time located on an open lot surrounded by flat terrain. The nighttime lighting obscures Chase and Charlie, who drop off Mason from the back of a station wagon after offering him a joint. His 'one last hit' indicates that they have easily proceeded to heavier drug use than the cheap beer of the year before, and in another affirmation of his higher status, Mason appears to have a possible girlfriend, whom he kisses as he leaves the car. (Her transient anonymous presence is all but trivial, though, as she is barely seen and is never mentioned again.) As we soon learn, Mason has started high school, and this is the eve of his fifteenth birthday, so the long hair he now wears also proclaims a certain independence, if not the same response to his mother's new marriage as he had with Bill years earlier.

Mason further exhibits his burgeoning shrewdness by asking his girlfriend for a piece of gum, conscious of his breath from smoking and drinking. This subterfuge all but immediately collapses when he enters the house to see his mother and her friends – including Jim – engaged in political banter and drinking wine. Before Olivia detects Mason's impeaching odor, Jim is actually the first to wish him a happy birthday, although this is preceded by a mildly accusatory question about the time (since it is now after midnight), suggesting that Jim is already critical of the boy's behavior. After Olivia hugs Mason, she casually asks if he's been drinking, to which he even more casually responds, 'Have you?' Turning fifteen and entering high school have obviously given him some guile as well as aplomb, as he initially admits to drinking 'a little bit,' and then admits the same when she mimes smoking a joint.

Unlike the transition to Year Three that introduced the marriage of Olivia and Bill, here Linklater inserts Jim into the story more indistinctly; there is no suggestion of a wedding, honeymoon, or an official marriage. In fact, Linklater suspends any mention of Jim as a legitimate husband to Olivia until two years later in the story, after she has separated from him, leaving unclear whether they exactly married or whether the marriage itself was so negligible as to not warrant formal designations.[4]

By the next day, however, Jim's role as a new surrogate father to Mason and Sam emerges when Dad shows up and not only brings a new wife, Annie (Jenni Tooley), into the story, but also a new baby son, Cooper (Landon Collier). As we quickly surmise, the relatives are not new to each other, because

Sam is familiar with her new little brother, as Annie is with her new stepchildren. Meanwhile, Jim makes small talk with Dad, telling him about Mason's interest in photography and commenting on home repairs, sounding every bit settled into his role as man of the house. (See Figure 4.3.) By contrast, Olivia is the one concurrently dealing with a home repair, as she talks with two Hispanic plumbing contractors about a broken pipe on the side of the house. After she agrees on the renovation with the apparent leader of the duo, Olivia displays the sincere interest she has in education, telling him, 'You should be in school. . . . Go to night school, at community college. It's pretty affordable.' Linklater may have placed this scene in the script as a mere example of Olivia's altruism, yet as we later learn after Mason's graduation from high school, the gesture represents her capacity to create positive and unexpected impacts beyond her roles as a mother and teacher.

A new character that *is* met with some surprise by Sam and Mason is the minivan driven by their father, which they enter with Annie and Cooper for a long ride to Annie's parents elsewhere in Texas. The incongruity of seeing his father driving a minivan prompts Mason to ask about the emblematic GTO he's accustomed to, prompting one of the most uncomfortable exchanges in the film, when Dad explains that he sold the muscle car to buy the present domestic carriage. Mason grows quiet and then explains to Dad his long-standing belief that the GTO would become his at sixteen, based on his lucid memory of a passing comment his father made seven years earlier. As we age, the varying values of remembrance come into stark effect, which

Figure 4.3 Mason is moved between the worlds of parental figures like Dad, Jim, and Olivia as he becomes an adult himself

are so inconsistently shared among people. In this case, Mason is confronted by the clashing priorities of adulthood and youth: Dad does not recall such a comment, plus he further denies he would have ever said it, and worse yet, he dismisses its significance to his son:

> Look, you can sit there like there's a death in the family, all right, but bottom line is that was my car.... I'm sorry if you had other ideas about it, but when you get older, you can save up and buy a car of your own, and be cool like I used to be. Or, you can get a minivan.

With this last sentence, Dad not only lays out to Mason the responsibilities awaiting him in adulthood, he is declaring his own acceptance of the parental responsibilities of middle age that he resisted as a young parent to Mason and Sam. The 'coolness' that Dad once enjoyed, and Mason now takes for granted in himself, is a transitory commodity, like the GTO, and even like youth.

In an effort to break the lingering tension, Dad presents Mason with a birthday gift that he calls 'The Beatles Black Album,' a set of CDs he made himself from solo work by each Beatle after their 1970 breakup. What on the surface seems like a mere eccentricity revealing Dad's taste in music is really a metaphor for the family, as he explains the way each member of the former band has individual qualities that 'start to elevate each other' when they are put together. He passionately proclaims, 'There is no favorite Beatle! . . . It's in the balance,' and then goes on to exemplify their peculiarities ('. . . George, who talks to you about God; John is just, "No, it's about love and pain" . . .'), making a case for their synergy as individuals who form more than the sum of their parts.[5]

Linklater slyly punctuates this conversation with a sound bridge to the next scene that contains the leisurely opening bars from Paul McCartney's hit 'Band on the Run' from 1974, a song about a band trying to escape from their past.[6] This new family band then arrives at the rural home of another family, Annie's parents, Cliff (Richard Jones) and Nana (Karen Jones), who greet the contingent warmly outside of their modest ranch house. They all soon gather in the living room to present Mason with a birthday cake adorned with candles, and the presents that follow are loaded with satirical significance.

First Nana gives Mason a Holy Bible, since 'I heard you didn't have one.' If this gesture wasn't already awkward enough, she has had the book inscribed with his name on the cover and points out the red-letter aspect of the print, which 'means that everything that Jesus said is in red.' Religion has held absolutely no presence in Mason's life to this point, despite the prominence of Christian doctrine in Texas, and his mildly befuddled reaction to the book intimates his ongoing disinterest. This character quality is actually in keeping with American teen films at large, which rarely label any protagonists with religious identities, notwithstanding the substantial portion of youth, particularly in the south, who are active church members.[7]

Dad and Annie then give Mason a more practical (yet no less symbolic) set of clothes: a dress shirt and tie with a matching jacket. Lest his son view the gift as too stodgy, Dad explains, 'You've got life ahead of you. . . . You've got dances, and job interviews.' The attire is one of the brashest loaded signs of encroaching adulthood in this film about boyhood: this is the dress of older men who have 'life ahead' of them, such as the rituals of acquiring partners (at dances) and careers (at job interviews).

Then Linklater concludes the litany of implications with the most extreme item yet, when Cliff stands up to proudly bestow upon Mason a 20-gauge double barrel shotgun. Like religion, guns are also customary in Texas culture, even though neither has previously factored in Mason's life, and given his interests, he has no use for either. The theme running through this gesture is not about spirituality or practicality, though, but rather masculinity, as Cliff makes clear: 'My dad gave it to me when I was a little younger than you, and his dad gave it to him. Well, you're fifteen and I'd like for you to have it, all right?' There is thus a patriarchal lineage enacted in this exchange, with Mason inheriting the phallic tool of older men, men who apparently lived by a masculine code unlike his own father, who has instead given him an urbane uniform (and that arty gift of music). Cliff emphasizes the paternal obligation that comes with the gun, telling Mason he will help him learn the weapon, another suggestion (along with the Bible) that these new in-laws, not unlike Bill before, have a very different set of priorities from his existing family. Dad later mentions to Mason that Olivia would not approve of the gun, and the familial disparities that Mason endures are again manifest.

The family next proceeds to put that gun (and others) to use, shooting targets outdoors at some presumably nearby location. Dad's and Cliff's instructions to Sam and Mason indicate that the kids have likely never fired guns before, and their moderate success at hitting targets prompts Cliff to ask Mason how he felt in shooting a tossed piece of wood, anticipating it should be quite rousing. The boy quietly responds, 'Felt good,' yet there is no greater aggressive release forthcoming. As we have previously seen, Mason finds power in thought and reflection, not emotion and action.

That evening, the entire group has gathered on the front porch to hear Dad play guitar to an unnamed composition (identified in the credits as 'Ryan's Song' and written by Hawke), to which Annie and his children sing along.[8] As with all of Dad's performances, the lyrics comment on the story, in this case about a narrator who bemoans the dilemmas of making life choices with contrasting consequences. Mason sings one line that could be his personal motto – 'Consider everything deeply, but still remain fearless' – and a subsequent line of resignation: 'If I don't try, I'll never fail.' Once again Linklater has provided his protagonist with subtle statements about the strains of his development, which is full of ambition and doubt, connection and isolation.

The director reserves another heavy commentary on Mason's mental state for the subsequent scene of the family attending a small church service the next morning. Wearing his new business suit, Mason passively listens to the preacher as he reads from the Bible about the infamous doubting Thomas, who would not believe Jesus had returned from the dead until he could see and touch him. The preacher recites the verse, 'Blessed are those who can believe without seeing,' meant to apply to religious faith, a faith that Mason does not appear to have. The scene cleverly conjures comedic tones for its display of Mason's exasperated performativity, adorned in formal attire that he would otherwise resist, listening to a message about a religion he does not follow, and yet attending to these family obligations without complaint.

Lest the pressures of this moment pass without release, soon thereafter Mason and Sam accompany their father and Annie on a walk to a pond, where Dad asks his teenage kids if they would return for baby Cooper's baptism. They agree, though prompting Mason to ask if he and Sam were baptized. Dad's snickering response speaks to his temerity as a younger man: 'I wasn't the least bit concerned with the state of your soul.' Now, however, with the expectations of Annie's family to respect, Dad at least accepts the ritual, giving further pause to his older children, which Sam finally questions: 'You're not becoming one of those God people, are you, Dad?' Rather than answering – after Annie gracefully intones that she is hearing this – Dad pivots to another signifier of the difference they have from Annie's folks, telling Mason that the shotgun would be better kept by him. Indeed, Dad recognizes the differences he is absorbing for his new family that will not be shared with his previous family, an important example for Mason to observe as he is on the verge of establishing serious new relationships without the presence of his own family.

Year nine [1:43:16–1:54:00]

Mason is about sixteen in the fall of 2011. The story action takes place on a Friday afternoon and evening.

1   A teacher gives Mason a talk about ambition and art in the school darkroom.
2   Jim gives Mason some cold advice about being cool [later that day].

3   Mason takes pictures at a high school football game [that night].
4   Mason approaches Sheena at a party and they go off to talk [later that night].
5   Jim confronts Mason about his sense of time [later that night].

A somewhat serious relationship is exemplified in the next scene, when Mason has his first extended discussion with a paternal figure who is not one of his parents, his photography teacher Mr. Turlington (Tom McTigue). The time lapse to another year is most noticeable by Mason's shorter hair, and the entire scene is filmed in the typical red light of a darkroom setting, giving the dialogue a dramatic ambience.

Turlington berates Mason for spending too much time in the darkroom and not on his assignments, giving Linklater an opportunity to make a subtly crafty criticism of media: after the teacher lists the digital projects that are due, he points out that Mason doesn't even need to be in the darkroom, implying that the expediency of digital photography is making his printmaking endeavors obsolete. Remarkably, we see few of the results of Mason's photographic work until his senior year, when he is taking down pictures of the girl who has by then broken his heart, so his occupation with tangible images speaks to a longing for permanence that photography itself deceptively promises and yet denies.

The greater import of the scene is Turlington's attempt to offer some 'tough love' to the talented but unregimented artist, as he emphasizes that talent alone will not carry Mason without 'discipline, commitment, and a really good work ethic' – the kind of restrictive qualities that many teenagers find stifling. Mason does not take the criticism without some self-defense, claiming that he does work hard at taking numerous pictures, which prompts Turlington to give him an assignment that he will dislike: photographing the school football game that evening. Further, the teacher rattles off a list of requirements, and then exhorts Mason to envision what he wants to do. When Mason responds that his real ambition it to 'take pictures, make art,' Turlington drolly quips, 'Any dipshit can take pictures, Mason. Art, that's special. What can you bring to it that nobody else can?' And not wanting to miss the possible significance of his advice, Turlington closes by suggesting that Mason might look back with appreciation for this conversation.

The pretense of magnitude here may seem disconnected from the many quotidian moments throughout the rest of the film, but of course Linklater is also suggesting that Mason may *not* remember this conversation, and Turlington's efforts may be in vain. More important is the fact that Mason is brought to mull over his goals, particularly in relation to his art and work, which he has not been made to articulate in any previous scene – he is now starting to claim some ownership for his actions. This progress becomes even clearer in conversations he has as the day, and years, go on.

A brief scene then introduces the next significant friend Mason will have in his final years of high school, Nick (Sam Dillon), who teases him about the long time he was in the darkroom with Turlington. The homophobic discomfort inherent in this jab, which is unfortunately typical of many teenage boys, carries into the next scene that afternoon when Mason sits down in the kitchen with Jim as Sam and Olivia prepare dinner.

Now attired in a correction officer's uniform, Jim looks haggard as he opens a beer, having apparently settled into a dreary job and a defeated role within the family, demonstrated when he castigates Sam for using the word 'shit.'[9] Jim's duty as a moral guardian carries over to a sarcastic comment about Mason's fingernails, which 'some girl' at school painted blue that afternoon. Mason's lax interest in his appearance does not concern Jim, but his gendered status does: 'Last summer it was the earrings, and now the nails. You got a . . . purse to go with all that?' In contrast to Nick's jokey comments earlier, Jim expresses serious sexism and homophobia; Mason's supposedly feminine traits goad him, plus Mason is not 'cool' like Jim was in high school, specifically because he does not have a job. Ann Hornaday (2014) expresses another likely tension within the militaristic Jim, which is that Mason's affectations suggest 'that he's dodged at least most of the misogynist conditioning of a boy's life.' Jim has thus quickly become another cautionary example for Mason, unable to find decent work to apply his skills, and conflicted by any feminine qualities that threaten to compromise the gender roles in his insecure relationships. Certainly Olivia earns more than he does, but finds herself selling items online because they are 'house poor,' as she says. In many ways, Jim is the opposite of Bill – younger, poorer, nonprofessional – and yet similarly remains a deficient role model. Where Mason found Bill's arrogance assaultive, he now finds Jim's anguish alienating.

The next scene actually features Mason working, albeit unpaid, as he takes photographs at the football game that Mr. Turlington assigned. His obligation to labor is nonetheless emphasized again, when Nick brings a message from the teacher to 'cut the artsy crap and shoot the game.' Mason not only resists his given orders, he has been seeking out more compelling aspects of the action. This may be impractical against the circumstances, yet suggests his longing to find significance beyond the obvious.

Nick also provides a transition to the next scene that night, having mentioned that he has secured them a ride to a party, where he then appears as the drummer in a student band. While a multitude of teens (including Sam) mingle and drink, Mason casually nudges a girl who we will later know as Sheena (Zoe Graham), his first lasting girlfriend.[10] The conversation that

Figure 4.4 Sheena is an understanding listener when Mason shares his thoughts

follows between the two of them is the richest sustained dialogue Mason
has in the film to this point, as he valiantly tries to explain his sincerely
sophomoric views of his life (see Figure 4.4).

Linklater emphasizes the intimacy and importance of the scene by shooting in close-ups as Mason and Sheena sit alongside each other and awk-
wardly waver toward touching. Mason opens with an existential statement
about his work (and art): 'I just feel like there are so many things that I could
be doing and probably want to be doing that I'm just not.' He then hesi-
tates as he admits that he reluctantly cares about what other people think,
a profound realization for any socially developing adolescent, particularly
an equable rebel like Mason. He complains of the way people 'control'
him without knowing it, and Sheena counters with the question of how he
would be different 'in this perfect world where no one's controlling you'?
Of course, Mason has a sense that it would be much better 'to do anything I
want, because it makes me feel alive,' yet further admits that he also doesn't
know just what 'normality' really means.

Sheena's attentive glances and soft delivery already indicate her affection
for Mason, and then she delivers a provocative compliment: 'You're kinda
weird, you know that?' With this sentence she is able to simultaneously point
to his charm and disarm his diffidence, leading him to confide, 'I really like
talking with you. I don't usually even try to, like, vocalize my thoughts
or feelings or anything.' This is an important declaration for the artist as a
young man, who naturally warms to the pretty girl's challenges much easier
than his teacher or stepfather. Mason will find in Sheena a confidant as well

as a muse to inspire him, before she becomes an antagonist who frustrates what he comes to believe. He is indeed searching for an image, of his girl-friend and of his adulthood, because 'words are stupid,' as he murmurs to her. When Sheena concludes the scene by smiling at Mason's comfort with her – before any first kiss, in keeping with Linklater's agenda – she quietly seals his ardor.

When Mason returns home that night, he is not prepared for the waiting Jim to unload one more conflict in this challenging day. After Mason casu-ally apologizes for being late, Jim, who is clearly finishing off another of multiple beers, expresses his scorn at Mason's indifference to Olivia (and, by association, himself), and begins barking complaints in a militaristic tone that is understandably familiar to him. When Mason wishes he had a day 'where everyone isn't all over my ass,' Jim seizes upon the mildly homo-erotic remark by rising up from his chair to face the boy, taking another stand by asserting that 'If you wanna live in my house, then you get home when you say you're gonna be home.' Having reached his limit, Mason responds with a clarifying insult: 'You know, Jim, you're not my dad.'

Jim's reaction once again points to his own self-contempt, as he boasts, 'I'm the guy with the job, paying the bills, taking care of you, your mom, your sister . . .' Only he now views this 'care' as financial rather than emo-tional, having never connected with anyone in the family in a meaningful way. When Linklater closes the scene with Jim reiterating, 'I'm *that* guy,' his criticism of Jim is complete. Jim is indeed that guy who, like Mason Sr., took on more responsibilities than he could manage at an age too young for redemption. Bill, by comparison, came to dismiss his responsibilities after growing too assured in his authority, and fell beyond redemption. Faced with these three failed fathers, Mason is left with understandable concerns about his own manhood, and ultimately he will embark on his adulthood without any of them present to 'control' him.

Year ten [1:54:01–2:10:51]

Mason is going on seventeen in eleventh grade during spring 2012. The story action takes place over two days.

1 Mason talks with Olivia as she rues her house expenses.
2 Mason drives to work in his modest pickup truck [later that day].
3 Mason flirts with a girl at his job, and his boss badgers him [later that day].
4 Mason talks with Dad by videophone as he plans to visit Sam [later that day].
5 Mason and Sheena drive to Austin and talk about technology [later that day].

6   Sheena asks Sam about college while Mason shoots pool [that night].
7   Mason and Sheena listen to a band with Sam and her boyfriend [later that night].
8   Mason and Sheena talk about college life at a diner [into the next morning].
9   Mason and Sheena walk around Austin until the sunrise [that morning].
10 Sam's roommate finds Mason and Sheena in her dorm room [later that day].

Changes that were possibilities in the previous year are now realized the next year as Mason has a job, a car, and a girlfriend, plus Jim has left the family. The story returns to the familiar confines of the family kitchen, where Olivia is now seated alone at the table working through a bothersome stack of bills. She quickly signals Jim's departure by telling Mason she would like to sell the house because it has grown too expensive, relaying with middle age wisdom, 'I've spent the first half of my life acquiring all this crap and now I'm gonna spend the second half of my life getting rid of all this stuff.' She all but immediately applies the comment to the 'couple husbands' she has surpassed, suggesting the accumulation of burdensome commodities in her life has been romantic as well as financial.

In the space of a moment across the next two edits, Linklater reveals Mason's new place in the workforce (he is a dishwasher at a local restaurant) and his new status as a driver, although his small used pickup truck is a far more practical ride than his father's old muscle car. These markers of his increasing independence are then followed by the decidedly adult banter Mason swaps with a female co-worker, who teasingly offers to 'blow' him – although this is neither a girlfriend nor Sheena, signaling how he has grown comfortable with sexual candor since his days of boasting to buddies.

Actually, the more adult matter at hand is pressed by Mason's boss, Mr. Wood (Richard Robichaux), who barges into the kitchen to alert him to the dishes piling up in the dining room. Following the scorn he absorbed from Mr. Turlington earlier, Mason stomachs Wood's detailed but lightly mocking critique of his inattention to work, which ends with the ironic possibility of being promoted to fry cook. Mason's less than enthusiastic response betrays his recognition of the low station he occupies, and further highlights the difference between menial work that could be his fate (per Turlington's warnings) and the rarified 'art' that he wants to achieve beyond mere labor.

After returning home that afternoon, Mason talks to his father through a video connection on his phone, one of the few technological interventions that Linklater indulges for his teenaged protagonist. Mason is currently planning a trip to Austin, to visit Sam at the University of Texas, and Dad reminds him to submit his application to the school as well. Even though his application would be early (since Mason has yet to start his senior year), Dad persists with his paternal advice as he senses his son's usual lassitude: 'Let 'em know you're a man who knows what he wants. A little bit of decisiveness goes a long way in this life, all right?' Dad is still proud that Mason is working, and proud of his younger son Cooper, whom he shows off with Annie, but before closing, he can't resist offering more advice to Mason on safe driving. Dad continues to balance his presence (even through media) between his first family and his second, much the way that Mason is learning to balance the different interests (work, school, romance, friends, family) in his own life.

Before Mason departs, Olivia asks him about his arrangements in Austin, and while undetectable at the moment, he lies that Sheena plans to stay with a friend when they are there. Mason and Sheena will in fact spend the night out in Austin, and later sleep in Sam's dorm room, with no further mention of the 'friend' she would supposedly visit. The duplicity may be Mason's attempt to conceal his intimacy with Sheena, and Olivia hints that she already knows he may be lying. Olivia also exerts some parental pressure for Mason to attend to his homework, and jokes that she could come along on the trip, maintaining her latent presence as well.

By contrast, the rest of the night provides Mason with a sense of adult autonomy unlike he has enjoyed to this time. As he and Sheena drive to Austin in his truck, Mason reveals his thus far unspoken agenda to avoid dependence on social media, which has been evident in the film to this point (particularly in comparison to his real-life counterparts). His declaration is earnest: 'I just wanna try and not live my life through a screen. I want, like, some kind of actual interaction.' This is, of course, what he has desired with Sheena, and though she teases him by looking at her phone, he maintains his apprehension with a protest that evinces one of Linklater's central themes in the film:

> I know you're joking, but, I mean it's kinda true you have been, you know, checking your phone this whole time, and so what are you really doing? You don't care what your friends are up to on Saturday afternoon but you're also obviously not fully experiencing my profound bitching, so it's like everyone's just stuck in, like, an in-between state. Not really experiencing anything.

This mere experience of life is, of course, what *Boyhood* celebrates at every turn, and Mason's 'profound bitching' expresses the very lack of experience that so much current technological mediation engenders. Mason once again indicates his distinction from the typical teenager of the 2010s; although not to be too far removed from digital influence, Sheena quickly notices that

Figure 4.5 Mason and Sheena debate the merits of smartphone conveniences

a friend has posted a Facebook photo of her new pet pig (see Figure 4.5). Mason cheerily but sarcastically agrees with the consequence of the pig picture, 'That is a really cute, tiny pig. Our lives can go on.' Linklater leaves the scene with this pronounced tension between Mason's principles and his practices, another foreshadowing of conflicts that every adolescent faces between childhood and adulthood.

After they arrive in Austin, Sheena and Mason then get to experience some of the lifestyle that Sam now enjoys with her unnamed boyfriend. All four may yet be minors, which poses no prohibition to their shooting pool and drinking beer at a bar, and for a rare moment in the narrative, Mason is marginalized as Sheena asks Sam about her boyfriend and college life. Sheena exudes a bracing confidence about her decisions, claiming that she's going to pay her own way through college (although *how* is unclear), and Sam responds with oblivious naiveté, 'You don't have to listen to your parents after you turn eighteen. I mean, especially if they're not helping you financially.' Such hubris is gloriously aspirational for a young adult.

The quartet continues into the Austin nightlife, noticing performers on the street and stopping by a club to hear a band.[11] Linklater once again maintains meaning in the supposedly mundane, as the lyrics from a song by the band, Austin Steamers, sound an ominous alert to these youths, starting with, 'On the day that I was born I started growin' old,' and closing on the portentous, 'Hard livin's gonna be the end of me.'

Mason and Sheena are not exactly living hard just yet, although they stay up the rest of the night until the dawn, stopping at a local restaurant to take in the atmosphere they anticipate will surround them in a little over a year.

The occasion provides Linklater with an opportunity to pay homage to his own *Slacker* through the character of a man speaking to himself, representing one of the eccentric denizens of Austin whom Mason and Sheena find amusing, particularly since Mason has the impression the man is a professor from the university. Strikingly, Mason's typical sangfroid – expecting that college life will mean 'staying out all night and going to shows' – soon becomes more circumspect:

> I don't know, doesn't it all seem a little overwhelming? I mean, college? I mean, I like the idea of being away from home and gaining skills and getting better at photography. I just, I don't know, I'm not counting on it being some big transformative experience.

Mason's cynicism, he explains, is informed by the fact that Olivia still seems 'just as fuckin' confused as I am,' despite her degrees. Indeed, Mason continues to face recurring frustrations about the expectations for his life, which he realizes are vague despite their supposed order. After all, his is a generation heading off to college with full awareness that the cost of their higher education (and the debt that comes with it) may not justify the marginal increase in lifelong income that it presumably promises. His current photography skills are likely enough to earn the same meager salary he would gain from any liberal arts diploma, and he has no other ideas for career pursuits that his college years might yet beget. His best hope, which he already disregards, is that college may indeed be a 'big transformative experience' beyond the middle-class aspirations of job security that have been ascribed to it in recent generations. He may manage to maintain some levity in his lamentations, though Mason already knows that college is just another moment in his ambiguous trajectory through life.

This ambiguity aside, Linklater continues to commemorate the quiet moments of evolution that Mason enjoys, as he walks across the streets of Austin in the early morning hours with Sheena, finding a parking garage from which they watch the sun rise as they tenderly embrace. The morning light reveals that the comfort the young couple share is affectionate yet also fleeting, and the silence surrounding the two of them is equally special yet ephemeral. These scenes capture Linklater at his most poetic within the film.

The suggestion of serenity is then broken with an edit revealing Sam's roommate returning to her dorm room later that afternoon to discover Mason and Sheena in bed together. The cold light that now shines into the room, coupled with the embarrassing arrival of the roommate they did not expect, make the two recoil under the bedsheets. Here is a sample of the real college life they perhaps do not relish, the cramped and compromising nature of dorm lodging, reminding them that they are not alone, emphasizing the expanding accountability that accompanies their independence.

Year eleven [2:10:52–2:30:24]

Mason is about eighteen and finishing high school during spring 2013. The story action takes place over several indeterminate days.

1   Mason takes down his photos from a school exhibit and talks with a teacher.
2   Mason argues with Sheena about the prom and their breakup [later that day].
3   Mason returns home from graduation to a family party [different day].
4   Dad consoles Mason about his breakup with Sheena [that night].
5   Olivia explains her next move to Mason and Sam over lunch [different day].

The closing of Mason's high school experience is in many ways just as uneventful as the rest of his schooling, although Linklater provides further signs of his protagonist's hardening attitude as he moves further into adulthood. The first such demonstration is his removal of large photos from a school exhibit, each of which features Sheena in striking poses. While the audience is not yet privy to the status of their relationship, Mason's pause of ambivalence before he begins removing these artistic images foretells the grief that lies ahead.

A teacher approaches Mason to congratulate him on winning a 'silver medal,' a compliment that he calmly recognizes, along with her remark that he earned a college scholarship. This passing reference to Mason's financial status – to which he replies, 'Every little bit helps, you know' – is one of the few articulations of how class affects him, despite how he has grown up under clearly meager means. Even after his tenuous years with Bill as a father, during which he lived in a bigger house with more space and stuff, Mason maintained humility about class atypical of many teenagers, who can often be fashion conscious and materialistic. As he goes on to explain to the teacher, he still plans to work over the summer 'to save up some money' before heading to school, a prudent plan.

After the teacher suggests to Mason that he might be feeling the 'voluptuous panic' of going to college, she adds a prescient insight, 'You kinda find your people in college,' a prophecy that we will begin to see unfold at the end of the film. The sentiment is met with immediate contrast when Mason is looking at a photo of Sheena behind a gauze sheet, illustrating her ongoing translucence in his life, and she sends him a text message:

'What's your deal? Meet me at the tree.' This tree without further reference may have once been the place where the couple met to share stories of their days, but now it is the setting of an argument, for they have become less of each other's 'people.' Their physical distance from each other highlights that they are already past a breakup, as Mason criticizes Sheena for telling her best friend that 'you're going to the prom with this *loser* even though you're not dating him anymore.' He is doubly dramatic here, in his tone and in describing himself as a loser, going on to jab Sheena by pointing out, 'we wouldn't be having this conversation [about the prom] if your college boyfriend weren't out of town this weekend.' The prom, that ritual of closure and celebration endemic to myriad American high schools, has thus been compromised for Mason, after he bought the tickets in anticipation of sharing the ceremony with Sheena, who has cuckolded him.

The scene is perhaps the most emotional moment in the film for the otherwise composed Mason, although he is still tightly coiled, barely repressing his anger at Sheena for moving on to another (older) boyfriend beyond him. He is at least able to clearly express his humiliation at the idea of attending the prom with his recent ex – calling himself 'King of the Pity Prom' – and Sheena relents to call off the plan. But the fight is not over. Sheena tries to look at the situation practically, sighing, 'We both knew this was coming,' until Mason snaps back that her solution to their stagnation was 'fucking some college guy.' Of course, as with all infidelity, Sheena's affair was merely a symptom of deeper frustrations, and she unloads yet another in the litany of disparagements that Mason has recently sustained: 'You know, it's actually kind of a relief not to have to be around someone who's so gloomy all the time.' Worse than merely cheating on him, Sheena has found a *better* alternative, and she insults Mason's natural demeanor in making her point.

With the hot coals of turmoil turning in his heart, Mason feebly tries to hurt Sheena in return, suggesting that he may have also 'been with' another girl. Alas, when Sheena pursues to ask whom, she calls his bluff, denying him what he really wants to hear: that such a transgression would matter to her. Sheena won't have Mason's brooding antagonism anymore, and she makes two painfully accurate observations as she walks away from him: 'This is pointless. Now you're just trying to be an asshole.' He has indeed *tried*, but her lack of interest has defeated even that effort, and Mason finds himself alone with his bruised pride.

Linklater does not linger on the bitter moment though, abruptly changing the scene to a much happier occasion as Mason drives home from a different ceremony, his high school graduation (though the sting of Sheena's actions will be manifest later). His friend Nick gripes that the festivities were painful, and Mason asks for a flask of liquor from him, amplifying his adult attitude that comes with a clear measure of danger. As they come upon

Mason's house and notice the number of cars parked outside for his party, he groans at the thought of so much attention and enlists the reluctant Nick in joining him.

The following scene – one of the longest in the film – is as close to a climax as Linklater will allow, with Mason encountering some of the characters we'd seen earlier in his life, now offering subtle commentary on his future. One new character in the picture is his father's brother Steve (Bill Wise), who interjects the appropriately awkward comments of an uncle, such as greeting Mason with, 'Get a job!'[12] Olivia quickly adds to the discomfort by asking Mason to pose in a picture with family, which is taken by Carol, whom we had not seen since Year Five (see Figure 4.6). Grandma Catherine, missing since Year Three, sounds another uneasy note by inviting Dad into the picture, saying, 'I'm feeling generous.' So much lingering family turbulence is elided and suspended in such comments.

Dodging any enmities, Mason turns to Carol and expresses his appreciation for her making the trip. Her daughter Abby (Cassidy Johnson), whom we have also not seen since Year Five, is now thirteen, and Carol remarks that Lee is on his senior trip, giving Mason pause as he realizes the time that has passed since he last saw them as a kid. Mr. Wood is next to approach him, and in another strained paternal gesture, he hands the new graduate something 'better than money,' a savings bond.[13] His considerate investment in Mason's financial future nonetheless gives him no modesty in commenting on Olivia's looks, continuing the suggestion that Mason is being

Figure 4.6 Carol takes a picture of the family on Mason's graduation day, with Mason Sr., Olivia, Catherine, and Sam

brought into a more mature status. That status is further intensified moments later, when Olivia's colleague Prof. Douglas, well into a few glasses of wine, suggestively asks Mason if he is single and needs a ride to college. The handsome young man, it seems, will have no trouble attracting women. Meanwhile, Olivia interrupts the party to offer a toast to Mason, stating with sincere optimism:

> I want to celebrate you and this next phase. And you're going to learn so much in college. You're going to have so much fun. You're going to have inspiring teachers. You're going to learn more about your art. I love you, babe. I'm so proud of you.

Dad, on the other hand, is not nearly so eloquent in his toast, commenting on Mason's efforts to find an in-state college they could afford. With some mild astonishment, Mr. Wood chimes in, letting Mason know that he could still work at the restaurant, a fate that everyone knows would be backsliding. Sam, whose presence in the film has noticeably declined, offers a noticeably inane sentiment when pressed to speak, slowly letting out, 'Good luck.' Mason seems relieved to avoid any further pomp beyond the circumstance, preferring to ruminate during his own time and on his own terms.

The more consequential dialogue in the scene actually occurs between the adults in Mason's life. First, Dad and Annie inelegantly reunite with Catherine, who goes on to express a duplicitous gratitude to Dad – 'I'm so glad you found her' – and then to Annie: 'You've got him at a good time, I think.'[14] Dad is polite yet unmoved, sensing insincerity in Olivia's mother, about whom he quietly comments to Annie, 'She's a bitch and a half.' Dad suffers an added gauche exchange with his brother Steve, who implicates Mason in their masculine pursuits through thinly coded boasting about their college years: 'If you're anything like me or your old man, you're gonna be pulling down some serious wool. You're gonna be tapping some masterful gap.' The impropriety of Uncle Steve parallels Dad's former mother-in-law, and neither of them seem to recognize the men their distant relatives have become.

The most striking interchange of the scene then takes place between Dad and Olivia, who find themselves alone in the kitchen. He tries to make light of the moment, asking, 'Am I your only ex at this party?' to which she adroitly counters, 'Yes. I'm not your only wife here, though.' Having made this reference to their present, Olivia reflects on the remarkable reality that their two teenagers are now both through high school. 'You did a great job with both of them, by the way,' Mason Sr. tells the mother of his children, eliciting her genuine surprise at his gratitude. She then points out that he's now doing it all over again, referring to raising Cooper, but his old ways remain: after offering to help pay for the party, Dad realizes he has no cash on him, and says he will get some from Annie's purse.[15] He may have matured, and may be more sensitive, but he is still not entirely responsible. Mason, by comparison, seems more aware of his obligations as he enters adulthood, continuing to exude his disdain for conformity.

The pensive mood permeating the occasion is not entirely missing from Mason, who visits his father that night at a club where his band will later be performing. (Here we also encounter another earlier character, Jimmy, who is shocked to see the older Mason after so many years.) Linklater cuts to the middle of their conversation, in which Mason has been bemoaning the demise of his romance with Sheena; now he can be candidly vulnerable in the confines of a bar with only Dad listening. The older man tries to console his son with sympathy, but after he suggests that Mason should not be 'crying over some silly girl,' the boy offers a revealing rejoinder, 'She wasn't a silly girl, though. I mean, she's a serious person. And I really thought we were . . .' The pain of young love is palpable in Mason's remorse, as his father tries to buck him up by pushing him to move on.

If the previous scene offered some educational culmination for Mason, the next few lines represent Linklater's intellectual epiphany for his protagonist. Advising Mason yet again on what would make him attractive to women, Dad offers with some bluster, 'You just gotta separate yourself from the pack in some way. Excel at something, you know, and then you have your pick of the litter when them front-runner hussies start sniffing around.' Of course, Mason has already begun to distinguish himself, which wasn't enough for Sheena, who didn't even like the pictures he took of her. Dad has heard enough about her, though, and makes a reference to Olivia, whom he felt stifled him and was not patient or forgiving enough.

Mason at this moment realizes that his parents' decisions have largely controlled his life so far, for instance, leading to the 'parade of drunken assholes' that Olivia dated or married. This was one of the themes that Linklater most wanted to explore in the film: children's lives follow the directions dictated by adults for so long, and then after the threshold of adolescence, they are expected to find their way on their own under the assumption that they somehow know how to be independent (Kiang 2014). This realization prompts Mason to ask the existential question, 'So what's the point?' At last, Dad makes a confident proclamation of vague reassurance:

> What's the point? I mean, I sure as shit don't know. Neither does anybody else, okay? We're all just winging it, you know? I mean, the good news is you're feeling stuff. You know? And you've got to hold onto that. You do. I mean, you get older and you don't feel as much. You're skin gets tougher.

As it turns out, for all of his remonstrations and advice, Dad does not know the meaning of life after all. What is more important, he stresses, is that Mason is moving from the dispiriting emotions of adolescence and into the equally uncertain though less upsetting wisdom of adulthood. Mason thus closes this graduation day with a tacit understanding that all of his 'profound bitching' may feel liberating and yet accomplish nothing.

Linklater then offers Olivia an opportunity to provide some perspective on her view of life when she takes Mason and Sam to lunch on another day. She has at last decided to sell the house and get rid of the clutter that has annoyed her, and alerts her kids to one more moving process they need to ride out. Sam maintains a familiar whiny tone, and Mason seems somewhat perplexed, but Olivia stands firm that she needs to make the move for herself. The mother's expedited efforts to avoid an empty nest are not entirely self-serving though, as she reminds them, 'You guys are adults. You need to take some responsibility!' No sooner than she makes this declaration, Olivia worries that Sam may be sick, when really she's just hungover, a sterling example of the irresponsibility that the mother is trying to eradicate in her offspring. This next relocation offers not just more opportunities for Olivia, it promotes more growth for Mason and Sam.

A manager at the restaurant approaches the table, who turns out to be Ernesto (Roland Ruiz), the contractor whom Olivia encouraged to attend school a few years earlier.[16] He explains that she changed his life with her advice, since he went on to college and is now enrolled at Texas State while he works at the restaurant. Olivia is all but speechless at her profound influence on this stranger, whom Linklater reintroduces as a demonstration of the supposedly random yet enormous impact people may have on each other without knowing it. More so, Ernesto's recommendation to Mason and Sam – 'You guys should listen to her. She's a smart lady' – endorses the parental effort she has made over all these years. Her children may not fully appreciate her sacrifice or her wisdom, although their reaction of quiet pause intimates that they recognize Olivia as a powerful force beyond their own lives.

Year twelve [2:30:25–2:39:37]

Mason is eighteen and on his way to college in late summer 2013. The story action takes place in one day.

1   Mason packs for college, and Olivia cries about how her life has gone by.
2   Mason heads out on the highway, taking pictures en route [later that day].

3   Mason meets his roommate, his girlfriend, and her friend Nicole [later that day].
4   The four go walking in Big Bend as Nicole tells Mason about herself [that evening].
    Closing credits [2:39:38–2:45:15]

Even though only a few months could have passed between the previous scenes and the start of this next sequence, Mason looks noticeably different since he is now sporting a goatee – he plans to start college with a new image. He's also in a new setting, packing up some of his things at his mother's apartment. Linklater introduces another commentary on the nature of people as Mason muses about the selection of his roommate, which was based on a computer survey of just 20 questions. He remarks to Olivia, 'Apparently we're not as unique as we want to think we are,' certainly a Linklaterian sentiment within his exploration of characters across so many films, and in this case, across an entire life so far.

While Mason seems excited at the probability of a 'pretty cool' roommate, he still hangs on to his critical suspicions of technology, surmising 'soon they won't even need a questionnaire, cause they'll just let the NSA scan your digital ghost.' Linklater juxtaposes this foreboding sense of the future with a token from Mason's past when he comes across the framed first photograph he took, which Olivia has packed among his moving boxes. His shallow dismissal of the gesture evokes a much more emotional reaction from Olivia than he expected. After a pause in which she is framed alone within the small space that is her kitchen and dining area and living room, Olivia begins to cry and exclaims, 'This is the worst day of my life!'[17] She continues with perhaps the most insightful monologue in the film, an overt exposition of mid-life crisis:

> You know what I'm realizing? My life is just gonna go, like that! This series of milestones . . . getting married, having kids, getting divorced, the time that we thought you were dyslexic, when I taught you how to ride a bike, getting divorced *again*, getting my Master's degree, finally getting the job I wanted, sending Samantha off to college, sending *you* off to college. . . . You know what's next? Huh? It's my fuckin' funeral![18]

In a matter of seconds, Olivia is able to sum up her life to this point, and realizes how fast it has all gone by. The moment is reminiscent of her grievance with Ted over eleven years earlier, when she confronted the sudden arrival of her adulthood while she was still enjoying her youth. Now later life is abruptly upon her (though she is still in her 40s), and her humble

surroundings signify the retiring future she faces. Curiously, we have witnessed very few of the milestones she mentions, because they are abstract
descriptions of events. Rather, we have watched her evolve in relation to
these events, if only by experiencing the moments in between them. The
same has, of course, applied to watching Mason grow, and by Linklater's
design, we studied his growth through the moments of life around those
milestones, not within them.

Mason is initially bemused at his mother's outburst and tries to lighten
her pessimistic outlook by asking, 'Aren't you jumping ahead by like, forty
years or something?' Indeed, Olivia may have much longer to live, yet she
is confronting the far more daunting prospect of what this change in her life
means: 'I just thought there would be more.' Such introspection and awareness of time is not the domain of youth, who see a less determinate life ahead
of them and are not taunted by the passing of life behind them.

Linklater lightens the mood and the gravity of the moment by cutting
to an expansive vista shot of Mason driving across Texas on his way to
college – the proverbial young man going west – under the strains of 'Hero'
by a band aptly called Family of the Year, a song that speaks of departure
and liberation:

> Let me go
> I don't wanna be your hero
> I don't wanna be a big man
> I just wanna fight with everyone else
> Your masquerade
> I don't wanna be part of your parade
> Everyone deserves a chance to
> Walk with everyone else[19]

This journey to his new life is Mason's opportunity to fight and walk on
his own, and along the way he stops to take unplanned pictures within the
increasingly barren landscape, preserving more selective moments. West
Texas is effectively desert, yet within this terrain he finds his oasis when
he arrives on campus (which goes unnamed in the film, although the scenes
were shot at Sul Ross State University in Alpine).[20] Mason locates his dorm
room and meets his roommate Dalton (Maximillian McNamara), who
immediately exudes a casual, easygoing vibe. Their surroundings are the
typical bland confines of most college dorms, and Mason makes clear that
he is not heavily invested in which side of the room he takes. He is, however, wondering about going to orientation, which Dalton boastfully dis-
suades him from attending: 'We got way better stuff to be doing, dude.' That
way better stuff is all but simultaneously suggested by the arrival of Barb

(Taylor Weaver), Dalton's presumptive girlfriend, who invites him to go hiking with them at Big Bend. Linklater consciously chose this location to recall Mason's childhood camping trips (Criterion 2016a), and in a further connection between his youth and his imminent adulthood, Mason meets Barb's roommate Nicole (Jessi Mechler) – who happens to have the same name as the girl who flirted with him after another momentous occasion, when he had his severe haircut in Year Four.[21] Barb offers a little more 'better stuff' by handing him a pot brownie that he promptly eats, claiming that 'It'll kick in when we get in the mountains.' In Mason's first few minutes at college, he is given ample evidence of how different the experience will be from his high school life: a new friend, a potential girlfriend, and free drugs are all readily presented.

What becomes the final sequence of the film begins in one of its largest locations, a canyon within Big Bend. Through casual chatter as they walk, Mason gets to know Nicole, who is an eager dance major and aspires to teach. The spacious range of terrain surrounding them further heralds the new journey they are taking, and Nicole's comments about child dancers are metaphorically related to this budding artistic couple as well: 'They have like no fear, and they're not self-conscious at all.' However, showing some of what he's learned, Mason responds, 'They haven't reached the awkward years yet.' Mason should know, since we've seen him flourish from fearless graffiti spray painting to talented pictures of a girlfriend who did not like the results, and along the way he confronted issues of control, discipline, and freedom.

Linklater has claimed (Kohn 2014) that he envisioned by the second year of production the last shot of the film, which finds his protagonist in a similarly contemplative state to when we originally encountered him, with the exception that he is now not alone (and supposedly high). While Dalton and Barb scream like coyotes atop a ridge, Mason and Nicole sit together with the twilight sun casting a warm glow on them. When Nicole asks how he is feeling, Mason responds, 'Great. Pretty great, to be honest.' The line may immediately respond to his drug-induced state, but, of course, it also suggests the comfort that he shares with her, a girl he can talk with very much like Sheena before.

Dalton, meanwhile, proclaims a more auspicious sense of the occasion off in the distance: 'This moment's having a multiple orgasm! It's like as if all of time has unfolded before us so we can stand here and look out and scream, "Fuck yeah!"' The ostensible nonsense of his stoned sensation is nonetheless an ironic inspiration to Nicole, who picks up the theme by asking Mason, 'You know how everyone's always saying, "Seize the moment?" I don't know, I'm kinda thinkin' it's the other way around. You know, like, the moment seizes us.' With this further Linklaterian observation, Mason

Figure 4.7 Nicole looks away as Mason gives us a last knowing glance in the final
shot of the film

agrees: 'It's constant. The moment, it's just . . . it's like it's always right
now, you know?'

And thus this moment hangs in infinite possibility, like the 'ceaseless
projections' Lethem (2016) perceived in the opening shot, as Mason quietly looks down and Nicole smiles his way, with both of them exchanging
and dodging furtive glances. All of life coheres around and constantly sepa-
rates from such moments, from every moment, and these two young people
are once again beginning to learn the imaginable impact – and apparent
entropy – of that reality. They may yet have a deep and meaningful relationship, or they may never meet again. (See Figure 4.7.) In many ways,
they are akin to Jesse and Céline from Linklater's *Before* films, yet even
before the first, as they are only starting the dialogue of moments that will
propel them forward.

Linklater holds this last moment in ambient stillness on screen for about
seventeen seconds before cutting to black, at which point the opening of
Arcade Fire's song 'Deep Blue' plays over the end credits. As with many
songs in the film, this choice goes beyond marking the time it was released
(which was 2010, a few years earlier), because the lyrics offer surprisingly
precise significance to the scene.[22] The introductory verse could be Mason's
own declaration on this exact experience:

Here in my place and time
And here in my own skin

I can finally begin
Let the century pass me by
Standing under the night sky
Tomorrow means nothing

The singer goes on to recount a memory from childhood, specifically in 1996 (just after Mason would have been born) when chess grandmaster Garry Kasparov was defeated in a match against an IBM computer called Deep Blue.[23] The chess match is emblematic of time changing in the eyes of a child, as the song goes on:

We watched the end of the century
Compressed on a tiny screen
A dead star collapsing and we could see
That something was ending

How fitting, then, that the closing shot leaves Mason in suspended animation on screen, at the threshold of his adulthood, once again pondering life under the wide firmament above, while the soundtrack expresses the greater global and universal transitions surrounding his boyhood.

Notes

1 Dad adds a further political dimension to the discussion by saying he read 'that although U.S. teenagers are not the most sexually active, we have the highest rate of teenage pregnancy.' Linklater may have been alluding to a specifically irresponsible aspect of Texas culture, because in 2008, 94% of school districts in the state taught abstinence-only sex education, in the face of the state sustaining one of the highest teenage birthrates in the nation. See Pollock (2017).
2 The realistic possibility of someone being hired now as a full-time professor of psychology by an American university with just a master's degree is virtually zero, although this implausibility is not addressed.
3 Hawke performs the song in the film, but it was written by Guy Clarke.
4 In addition to Olivia being inspired by Linklater's own mother (and named by Arquette in honor of her mother), the Jim character was inspired by one of his stepfathers, as he explained: 'When I was a kid, my mom was teaching a lot of guys who were Vietnam vets . . . and my mom actually ended up marrying one of those guys for a while.' See Criterion DVD (2016b).
5 The full playlist for 'The Beatles Black Album' – which grew out of a real mix of songs that actor Ethan Hawke compiled for his oldest daughter – is not only available, but so are the insightful and lengthy liner notes that Hawke revised from his original effort. See Hawke (2014).
6 For commentary on the song's meaning, see Landau (1997).
7 The most comprehensive research on religion among American youth has been published by Christian Smith, who speaks to specific regional aspects in Smith,

Denton, Faris, and Regnerus (2002). I also discuss the minimal presence of religion in movie depictions of American teens in *Generation Multiplex* (2014), p. 298.

8 An interview with Hawke about his musical contributions to the film can be found in Feinberg (2014).

9 Jim's position as a prison guard may seem a wry comment by Linklater on this ersatz father's role in the family, but it is another reference to one of his stepfathers who worked at the Hunstville prison. See Dawidoff (2015).

10 Lorelei Linklater's real-life boyfriend at the time is actually in this scene, drinking next to her. See Taylor (n.d.a).

11 Lorelei Linklater points out that Ellar Coltrane's real-life girlfriend at the time, Indica Shaw, played the hula-hoop dancer on the street in this scene; she is listed as 'Hooper' in the end credits. See Taylor (n.d.a). Bruce Salmon plays 'Guitar Player' alongside her; he is Ellar Coltrane's father.

12 Mason and Sam have two unnamed cousins in this scene, the daughters of Uncle Steve, who are played by Linklater's real-life youngest daughters, Alina and Charlotte. A character identified as 'Woman at Party' appears to be Steve's wife, and she is played by Genevieve Kinney, Ellar Coltrane's mother.

13 The U.S. Treasury had stopped selling savings bonds on paper at the end of 2011, so this gift from the boss – a prop that resembles an authentic bond before 2012 – is actually a historical anachronism.

14 There is an odd mistake in the Paramount DVD subtitles to this scene, which refer to Grandma Catherine as 'Aunt Jenny' at one point. Adding to the confusion are two lines in which the DVD identifies Mason Sr. calling Catherine by the name of 'Jen.' Nonetheless, this character is referred to in the script as 'Grandma,' and Mason Sr. calls her 'Catherine' earlier in the film as well as in the script; further, there is no end credit for an 'Aunt Jenny.' Linklater (2017) expressed confusion about this as well, offering a possible explanation: 'I think that might be a clerical error: her character on paper might have been originally named Jenny, but we shifted to Catherine right before shooting, and [maybe] that lingered on the page over the years? She's only "grandma" to the kids, so that's ultimately the credit. Definitely no "Aunt Jenny" around.'

15 Over all of the years his children grew to the age of eighteen, their father would have been obligated to pay financial support for them, which is never referenced in the film, although Dad does suggest that he is helping to pay for Mason's college in this scene.

16 Jaime Woo (2014) finds the characterization of Ernesto condescending and criticizes other racial aspects of the film.

17 Linklater explained that this line was lifted verbatim from producer Cathleen Sutherland's personal experience, on the day she dropped her own child off at college. See Buder (2014).

18 In addition to appropriating Sutherland's line for this scene, Linklater borrowed this profound moment from his own life, as he recalled: 'That image of Patricia sitting alone at the table when Ellar's leaving came from my own memory. When I left for college, [my mother] was just sitting at a table alone, smoking a cigarette. She seemed odd, and it took me years to realize it might be some emotional deal. Then when my own daughter [Lorelei] was leaving, I realized, *"Oooooh.* Now I understand." And I knew my daughter had no idea what I was feeling. She couldn't. She's 18. That's not the way it works. Parenting is a one-way thing.' See Whipp (2015).

19 'Hero' was the last song chosen for the film, and while Linklater felt it seemed a bit 'on-the-nose' in terms of referring to Mason after his breakup with Sheena, he thought the song suited the tone of this 'moment that needed a little bit of "too much" in order to work.' See Rothman (2014).
20 Even though Linklater included this first day at college for Mason, it also overlaps with the opening of his subsequent feature *Everybody Wants Some!!* in 2016, in which the protagonist starts college. When the film was still titled *That's What I'm Talking About,* Linklater said it is 'a continuation of *Boyhood*. . . . It begins right where *Boyhood* ends with a guy showing up at college and meeting his new roommates and a girl.' See McKittrick (2014).
21 Linklater comments in the Criterion DVD (2016a) audio commentary that he was conscious of naming Nicole after the girl who passed Mason a note in Year Four. He responded to my question about this (2017) that it could be read as a type of 'cosmic connection,' and added that there were 'lots of young ladies named Nicole in that generation,' plus he 'liked the echo' of the name. Her presence alludes to the potential fulfillment of that lost flirtation for Mason from years earlier.
22 For a somewhat grandiose yet quite interesting reading of the significance behind songs and other references in the film, see Schwartz (2014).
23 Linklater claims he 'begged' Arcade Fire leader Win Butler for permission to use 'Deep Blue' at the end of the film because its album of origin, *The Suburbs*, contained songs 'that influenced and infused their way into the last portion of the last several years of this movie.' See Taylor (n.d.b).

5 The moment of this boy's life

> When I was a child, I spake as a child, I understood as a child, I thought as a child: but when I became a man, I put away childish things.
>
> – I Corinthians 13:11

Boyhood debuted to the public at the Sundance Film Festival on January 19, 2014, in a special preview screening, which yielded the film's first professional review in *The Hollywood Reporter* the next day (Sundance 2014). Critic Todd McCarthy (2014) called the film 'a unique work in American cinema,' and though he expressed doubts about the film's future theatrical success, he concluded,

> The length suits the film's substance and the feeling at the end is of a rich, greatly rewarding experience. Certainly, Linklater, with all the other projects he pursued over the course of these dozen years, must have had his fingers crossed much of the time that this ongoing enterprise would work out all right in the end. It turned out as well, or better, than anyone could have logically expected.

En route to the limited commercial release that McCarthy anticipated, the film was screened at many other festivals, including the prestigious Berlin International Film Festival in February, which garnered Linklater a Silver Bear Award for Best Director. As the film circulated through further American festivals (Phoenix, Boston, Seattle) it gained progressive notoriety before screening in European markets over the summer. When *Boyhood* opened on a mere five screens in the U.S. on July 11, 2014, it had merited considerable advance interest, which was revealed by its enormous per-screen earnings of over $123,000 that week (Box Office Mojo n.d.).

Linklater had discussed his work on what had been 'The 12-Year Project' over the previous decade, and certain trade publications had stoked advance interest with some slight coverage of the production, but by summer 2014, the film had clearly generated the kind of critical appreciation reserved for Oscar contenders and classics. In mid-July, the *New York Times* called *Boyhood* a 'model of cinematic realism' (Dargis 2014), while the British *Guardian* had already labeled it 'one of the great films of the decade' (Bradshaw 2014). As the film continued to screen at numerous international film festivals, many critics were placing it on lists as the best film of the year. On November 30, *Boyhood* screened in the Museum of Modern Art's series known as *The Contenders*, which gathers films that 'will stand the test of time' for 'lasting historical significance,' which Linklater attended with Ethan Hawke, Patricia Arquette, and Ellar Coltrane (Museum 2014).

Audience interest in *Boyhood* became appreciable as well, especially given its low budget, lack of a star protagonist, independent production, very long running time, and maximum reach of 775 theaters in a week (by comparison, the highest-grossing film of 2014, *American Sniper*, screened in five times as many theaters). The film earned back its production budget of $4 million within its first three weeks of limited release, and by the time of its wider release in mid-August, it had earned $15 million. The film attained its greatest value within the audience it depicted, which the president of IFC Films, Jonathan Sehring, found heartening:

> It tested through the roof, but the place it really exceeded every expectation was young men, our hardest demo. We keep adding screens, and we have young people saying on social media that 'this is the movie of my life.'

> (Fleming 2014)

As awards season heated up toward the end of the year, *Boyhood* continued to play in theaters, even after its first DVD release on January 6, 2015. Due to the film's Golden Globe awards on January 11, where Patricia Arquette won as Best Supporting Actress, Linklater won for Best Director, and the film won as Best Drama, IFC again expanded the release of *Boyhood* in theaters. The film continued to play on the big screen through the Academy Awards in February, until ending its theatrical run after a remarkable 34 weeks with a total domestic box office take of over $25 million. While DVD sales garnered over $5 million, the international take for *Boyhood* was still larger, reaching nearly $32 million by 2016 (Nash 2017).

Linklater and his film would have enormous visibility through early 2015, as *Boyhood* became the most honored film of 2014. The movie received accolades through consortia large and small, including Best Film of the Year commendations by no less than two dozen film critics' associations, some being more predictable (Austin, Houston, North Texas, Oklahoma)

and some from farther-flung reaches such as Boston, New York, Los Angeles, Vancouver, London, and Toronto, whose group called the film 'a cinematic masterpiece that evokes beauty in life and the inevitable passage of
time' (Toronto 2014). Similar awards were bestowed by other groups with
wider range, including the Alliance of Women Film Journalists, the Broadcast Film Critics Association, the International Online Critics Poll, and the
American Film Institute, which issued the following statement:

> *Boyhood* frames the snapshots of a life lived, presenting an intimately
> epic coming-of-age tale unique in the history of the art form. . . . In a
> world consumed by 'selfies,' *Boyhood* looks outward to ask, 'Do we
> seize the moment. Or does the moment seize us?'
>
> (Matthews 2016)

If the critical praise for the film was effusive, Linklater and Arquette received
even more recognition, along with the core cast and crew.[1] In addition to
his directing awards at Berlin and the Globes, Linklater was named Best
Director of the Year by at least 30 critics' associations including the National
Society of Film Critics, plus awards groups including the Independent Spirit
Awards, while his screenplay was nominated for (or won) awards from over
30 groups, including a Best Original Screenplay nomination from the Writ-
ers Guild of America. Arquette was the most awarded member of the cast,
with Best Supporting Actress wins by no less than 40 groups, including
the British Academy of Film and Television Arts (BAFTA), the Screen
Actors Guild (SAG), and the Independent Spirit Awards. Other members
of the cast were not dismissed, though, as Ethan Hawke was nominated as
a Supporting Actor by the Golden Globes, the BAFTA, the SAG, and over
three dozen other groups; the ensemble cast was nominated by a half-dozen
groups including the SAG.[2] In addition to his role in the cast, Ellar Coltrane
was singled out as Best Young Actor by the Broadcast Critics Association,
and nominated for (or won) awards in other youth or 'breakthrough' categories from over a dozen groups, including the youth-centric MTV. The other
creative talent most honored for working on *Boyhood* was editor Sandra
Adair, who won the American Cinema Editors highest prize, the Eddie, for
Best Edited Feature Film (Dramatic), as well as many nominations from
other award groups.

Associations outside the U.S. were notably congratulatory for this
small American movie. In addition to the other BAFTA Awards, the British Academy of Film and Television Arts honored Linklater with its David
Lean Award for Direction. Best Foreign Film nominations (and wins)
would be bestowed by the Australian Film Institute, British Independent
Film Awards, International Online Cinema Awards, and the Irish Film and

Television Awards, as well as the awarding academies representing national film industries, such as Cinema Brazil, along with the Bodil (Denmark), César (France), David di Donatello (Italy), Fotogramas de Plata (Spain), and Guldbagge (Sweden) awards.

The highest level of prestige in the American film industry is, of course, represented by the Oscars, granted by the Academy of Motion Picture Arts and Sciences, where *Boyhood* was heavily favored to win after being nominated for Best Picture on January 15, 2015. At that point, the film was riding high from its Golden Globe wins just days earlier, as well as the numerous previous honors, but it faced stiff competition from seven other films nominated in the Best Picture category, each of which would win at least one other Oscar (a rare occurrence in Academy history). *Boyhood* entered the ceremony on February 22 with a total of six nominations, and in its one technical category, editing, Sandra Adair lost to the kinetic drumming spectacle of *Whiplash*. Linklater, nominated for Best Original Screenplay and Director, would lose in both categories to the film that went on to win Best Picture: *Birdman or (The Unexpected Virtue of Ignorance)*. Ethan Hawke, who had received his fourth career Oscar nomination, lost to J.K. Simmons as the tyrannical music teacher in *Whiplash*.[3]

The film's sole Oscar winner would be Patricia Arquette, who won Best Supporting Actress and took advantage of her moment on the Academy stage

Figure 5.1 Patricia Arquette delivers her cogent acceptance speech for the Best Supporting Actress Oscar at the 2015 Academy Awards

to address the country about gender issues beyond *Boyhood*: 'To every woman who gave birth to every taxpayer and citizen of this nation, we have fought for everybody else's equal rights. It's our time to have wage equality once and for all and equal rights for women in the United States of America' (see Figure 5.1). The plea was initially well-received by the liberal left, but *Variety* quickly reported that subsequent comments Arquette made in the press room after the show, in which 'she implied that gay people and people of color should throw their weight behind the issue [of equality] because of women's past support for civil rights issues, struck many as tone deaf' (Lang 2015). Indeed, this activist moment may have had a detrimental effect on her post-Oscar opportunities. While at age 46 Arquette was already slightly older than the average age of Best Supporting Actress winners (40), they have routinely enjoyed many plum starring roles following such a triumph; yet as of mid-2017, Arquette has only had one lead in a film after *Boyhood*, a low-budget mobster film (*The Wannabe*, 2015) that was never widely released (Merry 2016).

Boyhood remains one of the most critically acclaimed films of the past generation. The critics' compilation site, *CriticsTop10*, which tracks annual 'Top 10' lists by international critics, found the film on 536 of 802 such lists, and atop 189 of them, a record in their history of tracking back to 1980 (CriticsTop10 n.d.). Other critical compilations, by magazines such as *Sight & Sound* and sites such as *Metacritic* and *Rotten Tomatoes*, listed *Boyhood* as the best-reviewed film of 2014 (with remarkable scores of 100/100 and 98/100, respectively, at the websites). A 2016 BBC composite poll of 177 film critics from around the world who were asked to name the best films since 2000 ranked *Boyhood* as fifth (BBC 2016).

The quantity of these awards notwithstanding, the appreciation of *Boyhood* by critics may best foretell the quality of its further legacy with the public.[4] Claudia Puig (2014) of *USA Today* called the film 'an epic masterpiece that seems wholly unconcerned with trying to be one,' and remarked that 'it brilliantly captures the ineffable, bittersweet process of growing up, as seen through the prism of a child's lens.' Paula Mejia (2014) mused in *Newsweek*, 'If only for a few hours . . . *Boyhood* is proof that a strange magic can still bloom amidst the tragedy that buffets human life.' Stephanie Zacharek (2014) at the *Village Voice* poetically reflected on *Boyhood* as 'a cinema verité illusion of the endless days and nights of growing up, like a time-lapse movie of a flower opening up. It just so happens that this flower is a man.' Ty Burr (2014) began his *Boston Globe* review with an ontological perspective, '*Boyhood* may be why the movies were invented,' and concludes that the film 'is a stunt, an epic, a home video, and a benediction. It reminds us of what movies could be and – far more important – what life actually is.'

Linklater's accomplishment with *Boyhood* also elevated his status among critics, many of whom had enjoyed his quirky eclecticism but were now moved to grander assertions. Mark Kermode (2014) at *The Guardian* declared, 'What an extraordinary filmmaker Richard Linklater has become, a thoroughly modern rule-breaker with an old-fashioned sense of craftsmanship who provides the missing link between a twenty-first-century independent aesthetic and studio-era storytelling skills.' Ann Hornaday (2014) in the *Washington Post* compared Linklater to another rule-breaker, fellow Texan (and respected director) Terrence Malick, because their films are 'interested in philosophical questions about time and family and identity and consciousness.' Yet, she goes on to claim that 'unlike Malick's similarly themed *Tree of Life* (2011), *Boyhood* is free of fussy auteurist gestures and self-conscious grandiosity.' And after seeing *Boyhood*, Peter Rainer (2014) confidently proclaimed in the *Christian Science Monitor* that 'Richard Linklater is the most gifted director of his generation.'

After this barrage of impressive honors and praise, *Boyhood* seems certain to have earned a significant place in movie history that it will likely retain for generations to come. Yet what does the film ultimately tell us about boyhood, or childhood, at large? What are the salient statements the film leaves with its audience?

Compared to Hollywood products since the 1950s that eagerly exploited youth stories, *Boyhood* stands as a unique testimonial on the development of youth without fanfare or phantasm. Mason – his name suggesting he is a builder – is an unassuming signifier of Middle America in the early twenty-first century, maturing from pre-digital expressions of creativity to cynical hesitation at the future to come. His 'broken' family finds a way to cope through upheavals and reconciles their losses and differences. And Olivia emerges as the true hero, a single mother raising her children with meager means yet constantly improving herself, despite stumbles in her selection of male partners. If all families of divorce could ripen as fruitfully as Mason's – with both separated parents on good terms and in stably gainful careers, and both children well-adjusted into adulthood – American culture could be optimistic.

Boyhood ultimately asks us to not worry so much about the future, after all. Just as Mason marches through moments that are rarely planned and most often out of his control, such is life, which goes on regardless of us. For children growing up in the wake of 9/11, who no longer lived with the fear of global nuclear annihilation like their parents but instead felt the paranoid pressure of politicians and news media increasingly warning citizens that terrorism could be around any corner, the 2000s provided weak reassurance that their future was secure.[5] Mason initially enjoys an ascent to the supposed stability of middle-class family life only to see it collapse in a cloud of masculine arrogance and alcoholism, leaving him increasingly sardonic about his own opportunities in terms of relationships, labor, and society. His sense of identity evolves from embracing wonder to cautiously recognizing the corruption of power – in families, schooling, and even romance – despite hanging on to modest hopes.

Mason's identity, and the identity of childhood that the film explores, are important points to consider. When *Boyhood* began production in 2002, the concept of intersectionality had barely entered academic discourse, but by the time of its release in 2014, any critical viewing of the film, particularly with its encompassing title, would raise questions about the social traits of its protagonist and other characters. Linklater is clearly working from a white male heterosexual perspective, as embodied in Mason, and his lone demographic distinction in relation to most teens in other American movies and media is his working-class status, at least in the early and later years. He thus enjoys much automatic privilege that infuses the increasing frustration he feels about his thwarted expectations of life. (We glimpse this more in his sister Sam, who is given less screen time to express her vociferous protests.) By 2014, American youth had been elevated to far more conscious criticism of identity formations in relation to privilege and opportunity, so Mason's alignment with the dominant roles of race, gender, and sexuality can be viewed with a certain apprehension.

At the same time, the limitations of *Boyhood* in addressing a wider range of youth identities are motivated by Linklater's personal experience rather than an effort to normalize Mason's experience as universal. The director not only grew up in south Texas with many of the same experiences as his protagonist, but his view of youth is largely guided by a 1970s sensibility affiliated with his own childhood years: upward class mobility is upheld as a noble objective for those willing to work for it, race and racial tensions are all but invisible in social life, and sexuality is unquestioned by a culture that offers no alternatives to heteronormativity. For all of his sensitivity and critiques, not to mention his father's liberal opinions, Mason seems barely conscious of the homogeneity that characterizes the population around him. Like many children, he grows up with an inborn acceptance of his social status just waiting to be shattered as he becomes an adult.

The evolution of Mason's identity thus proceeds with little attention to his roles within culture and much more emphasis on his roles within personal relationships. *Boyhood* is actually filled with numerous demonstrable lessons for youth, each of which corresponds to persistent aspects of childhood, and is naturally unrealized until adulthood. These relate to familial permanence, creative expression, romance and resilience, social standing, and that recurring Linklaterian concern about the immediate and entropic passage of time. I hereby trace those lessons from the film in relation to Mason's identity development:

- Friendship is fleeting; family is forever.

From the first scene, in which Mason passionately explains the genesis of wasps to Olivia, until his departure for college, Mason relies upon his mother to recognize his interests and ambitions, and nevertheless remains unable to articulate the significance of this relationship. The final scenes find him with new friends at college after he has left his high school friends behind, and we anticipate that they will be influential, but they do not hold the formative relevance of Olivia and Dad. Even though Mason's sister Sam becomes a more marginal figure in his life as he ages, she continues to play the vital role of leading the way into adulthood, introducing him to college and providing a paradigm of dating that can be 'chill' rather than the high stakes he abided with Sheena.

As Olivia moves her kids across Texas, Mason's friends come and go, many with names that do not carry lasting impressions: Tommy, Lee, Kenny, Chase, Nick. Even his stepbrother for three years, Randy, is summarily discarded and forgotten, never mentioned again after Olivia leaves Bill – who is also never mentioned again – because they are not *real* family. Meanwhile, Mason's wastrel father reforms and becomes more reliable, maintaining a consistent (if sometimes distant) presence in his life, and he certainly has far more meaningful conversations with him than any of his friends. Olivia remains the rock, though, even if she crumbles a little in facing her own mortality. She gives Mason a model of determination and perseverance with little pressure, and when he leaves her nest at the end, he is clearly moving on with a sense of direction that is as poised and potent as his accomplished mother.

• Childhood interests are harbingers of adult pursuits.

The Aristotelian adage, 'Give me a child until he is seven and I will show you the man' – which inspired the British *Up* series – applies to our protagonist in many ways. When we first meet Mason at about this age, he is actively questioning life, finding unusual ways to foster his creativity (placing rocks in a pencil sharpener, spray painting in a tunnel), and wondering about the future of his family. For all his coolness, Mason has a lot on his mind. Linklater inserts small clues about Mason's further interests: in the fantasy worlds of *Harry Potter* that will factor into his questions about magic; in his quiet contemplations of a dead bird or his mother's contacts with new men that portend his uneasy understanding of life's changes; in the superficial attention he enjoys from girls that will eventually trouble his relationship with Sheena. Linklater's initial conception of Mason as a boy captivated by sports is all but entirely unrealized.

Rather, as a teenager Mason paints a mural the size of a wall as 'urban art,' he detests taking pictures of a football game, and his musings on magic become 'profound bitching' about the nature of technological influence. Linklater allows Mason's interest in photography to emerge rather organically, though, and does not labor to portray his early interest in visual design. Mason ultimately declines to take his first photograph to college with him, even though Olivia still regards it dearly, because he sees by that point how he needs to put away childish things. As his photography teacher suggests, Mason's talents may not be evident in his work ethic, but they emerge in his energy and exploration.

• Persistence in achieving goals will reap rewards; hard work pays off.

Although Mason may not have the discipline that one teacher would like to see, the student has many exemplars of achievement to guide him, starting with Olivia, and later his father. Both of his parents go back to school in their 30s to learn new career skills, and both become quite comfortable in their roles. Mason is initially frustrated by his father's decision to sell his old muscle car because he does not understand the greater benefit afforded by the practical minivan, which is Dad's destined symbol of accomplishment. Mason does not worry about grades at school; his concerns are in experience, not recognition. The same applies when he takes on his first paying job: he makes no mention of earnings or any need for money and overlooks the possibility of a supposed promotion because the position is only a means to his goal of leaving altogether. We learn about his college scholarship as he is tending to the photos that have demonstrated his talents, and thus Linklater makes the equation between Mason's productivity and his potential. Like most young people, Mason is still seeking direction on the eve of adulthood, and he now has the ability to find his way.

• Compromising personal goals for romantic security is problematic at best.

Given Mason's youth for much of the story, he does not find himself interested in any kind of romantic relationship until late in the film. Along the way, however, he is witness to Olivia's relationships with various men, including his father, which are all fraught with dilemmas that threaten to compromise her integrity. This is clear from Year One, when her current boyfriend Ted moans about Olivia's inability to go out socializing when she needs to stay home with her kids, and of course becomes only more intense as Bill becomes progressively abusive in their marriage. Granted, Bill's role as a college professor (and his financial stability) are likely motivating factors in her pursuit of graduate school, but she achieves her stature as a professor on her own terms after leaving that marriage.

Olivia's relationship with Jim also has its initial advantages – as a younger partner, he brings a certain verve to their new home together – yet before long, his own compromised integrity becomes a liability, and as with Bill before, his negativity affects the entire family, not merely Olivia. Crucially, Mason's final confrontation with Jim occurs immediately after he meets Sheena at a party, suggesting some of the confidence he feels in letting this fake father know that he is developing an adult identity of his own. Nonetheless, Mason is left to lament how his relationship with Sheena could not be sustained beyond its high school setting; her infidelity is inevitably with a college boy who offers more experience and less of the pessimism endemic to adolescence. When Mason later bemoans this breakup to his father, Dad tries to reassure him that Sheena did not represent the fulfillment that Mason anticipated, and we sense that this discovery will be the first of many Mason learns in his further romantic life. He and Olivia are both romantically uninvolved at the end, and yet both are better off in pursuing their interests on their own – though Mason is poised to take another chance on the moment with Nicole.

- Abuse is not worth tolerating.

The story obviously begins after Mason and Sam have shouldered the trauma of their parents' divorce, and while no suggestion is made that Dad was actually abusive toward Olivia, the references to their disagreements suggest that their marriage became painful to the point of dissolution. The first partner whom we properly see with Olivia, Ted, is aggressively insensitive to her situation as a single mother, and Mason watches him berate her, which foreshadows the resolve that Olivia will need to muster as she prioritizes her children over her own interests. She will be even more resolute in admonishing Dad when we first see them together, because she has already suffered his past negligence.

However, Bill introduces an altogether dangerous form of abuse far beyond mere disagreement. While his outbursts may be symptomatic of his alcoholism, his sober moments nonetheless reveal an authoritarian and malicious attitude toward Olivia and all of the kids. Initially, Olivia tries to leaven his critical approach to the children by expressing Bill's positive aspects, but within another year, his menace has become undeniable, and she strategizes her escape from him. A few years later, as Jim begins to augur a similar escalation to abuse, he is more easily discarded without nearly as much upheaval, because Olivia has grown more pragmatic and resilient. Linklater is not so moralistic as to suggest that Mason has become a child of abuse through his relationship with Sheena, which is generally affectionate, but his feeble resistance to self-pity in her betrayal of him does evince Mason's insecurity in the face of rejection. Like his mother, he will need to learn the limits of loyalty in accepting the distress that comes with every romance, and he will grow stronger accordingly.

• Graceful endurance of difficulty is an appreciable virtue.

Mason's breakup with Sheena is certainly not gracefully handled, in spite of watching his mother endure far more devastating circumstances in her failed romances. In fact, Olivia's growing abilities to overcome difficulties in her professional and financial life are in many ways overshadowed by the dramas of her relationships. Olivia manages to elevate her career status and the living conditions of her family through her distinct determination, overcoming the obstacles imposed by her meager means as well as the men who are intimidated by her conviction.

These triumphs seem somewhat lost on Mason and Sam, who, like most children, are preoccupied by their own interests, but we begin to see Mason's composure emerge in his teen years. He stoically resists bullies in middle school, he endeavors to fit in with his masculine cohort by boasting like his peers, he calmly resists Jim's criticism of him, and he stakes out – and succeeds with – his own artistic style, despite his teacher's reprimands over his lack of discipline. When he leaves for college at the end of the film, Mason does not wear the mantle of a survivor or a victim; rather, he remains ever the intrigued explorer, taking in his new experience (now with his camera) and joining others in the exploration of new possibilities. Mason endures the uncertainty of the future with a trust in the present moment that celebrates Linklater's overarching commentary on time.

• A cool disposition is a deceptive defense against disappointment.

Mason's demeanor is among the calmest of any teenager in American cinema history. His few outbursts of anger are even relatively tame, while his excitement in joyful episodes is usually tempered as well, which becomes more pronounced as he ages into a classically unemotional masculinity. For all of his composure, though, Mason still has sensitivity – to criticism, to embarrassment, and to rejection – that emerges after the fact, exposing his inner torments.

Mason's insulation is not a deliberate construction; rather, it seems to transform in a natural manner, as first he withstands the hostility of Bill, the disappointments of the family's many relocations, and the frustrations of young romance. He might swallow his contempt when Bill forces him to get his hair cut, or deny his pain when Sheena breaks his heart, until the impacts of these traumas emerge in more overt form later, usually with his parents. Olivia and Dad recognize their son's struggle to save face, which contrasts so dramatically to their daughter's penchant for protest, and they also soothe him when he turns to them with his true feelings. This is a pattern that Mason will clearly need to break after he leaves home, as he will face more disappointments in adulthood on his own.

• Politics and religion are weak forces of social unity.

Linklater has not been didactic in his films; if anything, his characters seem to discover meaning through often random and certainly inconsistent means. He does present Dad as a left-wing sympathizer opposed to President Bush and the election of John McCain, as a character who is himself sanctimonious in the beliefs he expresses to his children, but Mason's interest in specific politics is rather vague. Like virtually all teenagers, Mason and Sam are far more enchanted with the communal comportments of their friends and schools than they are by national events. The story cannot avoid politics though, as reminders are abundant beyond Dad's diatribes: Olivia's treatment by most men is patronizing, Jim is disillusioned by his role in the military, Mason detests the consumerist culture foisted upon youth, and their communities are awash in white pride. Within the conservative context of America (and particularly Texas) in the early twenty-first century, these conditions have been normalized, resulting in often unspoken recognition of social discord waiting to be exposed.

A more assertive yet subtle critique is reserved for religion in the film, specifically Christianity, as Linklater portrays his main characters within a largely secular milieu that belies the increasing divisions of devotion arising in post-9/11 American discourse. As jingoistic fears of Muslims gained traction, traditional Christian attributes became increasingly aligned with nationalism, a dubious development the religious right seemed to embrace even more after the election of Obama in 2008 (further evident in irrelevant accusations about the president's connection to Islam). The absence of religion for most of the film, despite the presence that churches have in almost all Texas towns, gives way when Dad sheepishly submits to the expectations of his second wife's parents in order to keep peace in his own home. Mason and Sam are clearly suspicious about his compliance, although they too consent to play along for the sake of propriety. Olivia espouses no religious beliefs whatsoever in the film, as do her two husbands after Dad. Religion is thus a repressive and ultimately extraneous force in the lives of these characters. Linklater's upbringing in Texas would have certainly informed his sense for how prominent Christianity is within the culture, yet his marginalization of the topic is a critique in itself. The negligible visibility of religion in the film and the minimal impact of politics reveal Linklater's deeper faith in the influence of humans as individual agents compared to their supposed social synergy.

• The enjoyment of life depends upon the recognition of its temporality.

Linklater's fascination with the passage of time finds its perfect articulation in *Boyhood*, and Mason is an ideal avatar in the search for understanding how we can best grapple with the absolute uncertainty and inevitable procession of time. The film in the end is a sampling of moments that demonstrate the ageless maxim of Kierkegaard (1843): 'Life can only be understood backwards, but it must be lived forwards.' As Mason discovers his increasing sense of agency in life, he is able to make more decisions on his own, and yet finds himself always already subject to the confines of family, geography, society, and reality itself. The numerous changes of his childhood, across homes and schools as well as friends, have given him a stoic appreciation for the present he occupies. Most of life makes little sense as it happens, despite the efforts of so much structure that society applies to time, such as the twelve years of organized schooling enforced on youth.

Mason does not flail in fury at any potential frustrations. He quietly recognizes the 'beauty in the mundane,' as Ellar Coltrane (2014) observed about his character. He respects the suspense that the future imposes, and, as a consequence, is better able to experience his time than so many teenagers who restively confront their development into adulthood. In recognizing the primacy of the present, Mason does not seek the epiphanic breakthroughs so pervasive within conventional youth depictions. On the edge of adulthood, he has come to terms with time and its inexorable changes at a level that some adults never achieve.

Of course, this wisdom is bestowed upon Mason through Linklater's own experiences and education over many more years than his protagonist has lived. If *Boyhood* was the work of a much younger author, it may have indeed expressed more anxiety about the nature of change and the inconsistency of life. Instead, Linklater has created a character with the advantage of age, evolving within a world carefully constructed as a work of art that simultaneously celebrates liberation from the demands of structure. *Boyhood* is at once a collection of mere moments, and a demonstration of how each of those moments may signify so much and so little all at once. That significance is thus unclear and its value is unreliable. All that remains certain is that we have this moment right now.

Notes

1 In a group interview, Linklater, Arquette, and Coltrane discussed the irony of being together more consistently during the one year of premieres and awards than they were during the twelve years of production. See Criterion DVD (2016c).

2 Curiously, even though they are apart and at odds through most of the film, Arquette and Hawke were nominated as Best Screen Couple of 2014 by the Women Film Critics Circle.

3 Ethan Hawke had previously been nominated for Oscars as Best Supporting Actor in *Training Day* (2001), and for Best Adapted Screenplay for *Before Sunset* (2004) and *Before Midnight* (2013), both of which he shared with Linklater and Julie Delpy, and in the case of the former, with Kim Krizan as well.

4 To be fair, there were a small number of negative reviews. Out of 276 critics listed on the review site *Rotten Tomatoes,* a total of 6 (2%) gave 'rotten' ratings, none of whom wrote for major publications.

5 As this book goes to press, Linklater is releasing *Last Flag Flying* (2017), which is a more overt examination of post-9/11 American perspectives with its story of a man joining two other veterans on a road trip to bury his son who was killed in the Iraq War.

Works cited

Adams, S. (2014) 'Interview: Richard Linklater Examines "Boyhood," Memory, Time & Perspective,' *IndieWire*, online, 15 July, www.indiewire.com/2014/07/interview-richard-linklater-examines-boyhood-memory-time-perspective-274507/ (accessed 20 June 2017).

Alexander, H. & Blakely, R. (2014) 'The Triumph of Digital Will Be the Death of Many Movies,' *The New Republic*, online, 12 September, https://newrepublic.com/article/119431/how-digital-cinema-took-over-35mm-film (accessed 20 June 2017).

Alter, E. (2014) 'How "Boyhood" Editor Sandra Adair Helped Shape the Film's 12-Year Evolution,' *IndieWire*, online, 17 July, www.indiewire.com/2014/07/how-boyhood-editor-sandra-adair-helped-shape-the-films-12-year-evolution-24211/ (accessed 20 June 2017).

BBC (2016) 'The 21st Century's 100 Greatest Films,' *BBC.com*, online, 23 August, www.bbc.com/culture/story/20160819-the-21st-centurys-100-greatest-films (accessed 20 June 2017).

Bibbiani, W. (2014) '*Boyhood*: Lorelei Linklater in a Therapeutic Interview,' *Crave*, online, 8 July, www.craveonline.com/site/720743-boyhood-lorelei-linklater-in-a-therapeutic-interview#/slide/1 (accessed 20 June 2017).

Box Office Mojo (n.d.) 'Boyhood,' *Box Office Mojo*, online, www.boxofficemojo.com/movies/?page=weekly&id=boyhood.htm (accessed 20 June 2017).

Bradshaw, P. (2014) '*Boyhood* Review – One of the Great Films of the Decade,' *The Guardian*, online, 10 July, www.theguardian.com/film/2014/jul/10/boyhood-review-richard-linklater-film (accessed 20 June 2017).

Buder, E. (2014) '5 Things We Learned about Filmmaking from Richard Linklater's "Boyhood",' *IndieWire*, online, 23 June, www.indiewire.com/2014/06/5-things-we-learned-about-filmmaking-from-richard-linklaters-boyhood-25035/ (accessed 20 June 2017).

Burr, T. (2014) '12-Year Journey into "Boyhood",' *Boston Globe*, online, 17 July, www.bostonglobe.com/arts/movies/2014/07/17/boyhood-gets-much-out-its-young-star-and-cinema-itself/yTixjbcHhCCOTKY2b8000I/story.html (accessed 20 June 2017).

Clark, A. (2014) 'Film of the Week: *Boyhood*,' *Sight & Sound*, online, August, www.
bfi.org.uk/news-opinion/sight-sound-magazine/reviews-recommendations/film-
week-boyhood (accessed 20 June 2017).

Coltrane, E. (2014) 'Growing Up on Camera,' in Lankes, M., *Boyhood: Twelve
Years on Film*, Austin: University of Texas Press, p. 12.

Considine, D. (1985) *The Cinema of Adolescence*, Jefferson, NC: McFarland.

Coupland, D. (1991) *Generation X: Tales for an Accelerated Culture*, New York:
St. Martin's Press.

Criterion Collection (2004) *Slacker* DVD, audio commentary track with Richard
Linklater.

Criterion Collection (2016a) *Boyhood* DVD, audio commentary track with Richard
Linklater et al., disc 1.

Criterion Collection (2016b) *Boyhood* DVD, *Twelve Years* featurette, disc 2.

Criterion Collection (2016c) *Boyhood* DVD, *Memories of the Present* featurette,
disc 2.

CriticsTop10 (n.d.) 'Best of 2014,' *CriticsTop10*, online, https://criticstop10.com/
best-of-2014/ (accessed 20 June 2017).

cummings, e. (1955) 'A Poet's Advice to Students,' *High School Spectator*, 26 Octo-
ber. Reprinted in Firmage, G.D., ed. (1958) *E.E. Cummings: A Miscellany*, New
York: Argophile Press, p. 13.

Dargis, M. (2014) 'From Baby Fat to Stubble: Growing Up in Real Time,' *New York
Times*, online, 10 July, www.nytimes.com/2014/07/11/movies/movie-review-lin-
klaters-boyhood-is-a-model-of-cinematic-realism.html?_r=0 (accessed 20 June
2017).

Dawidoff, N. (2015) 'Richard Linklater: About a "Boyhood",' *Rolling Stone*, online,
15 January, www.rollingstone.com/movies/features/richard-linklater-about-a-
boyhood-20150115 (accessed 20 June 2017).

Doherty, T. (1988) *Teenagers and Teenpics: The Juvenilization of American Movies
in the 1950s*, Boston: Unwin Hyman.

Driscoll, C. (2011) *Teen Film: A Critical Introduction*, New York: Berg.

Dunaway, M. & Wood, T. (2014) *21 Years: Richard Linklater* DVD, Breaking Glass
Pictures.

Feinberg, S. (2014) 'Three "Boyhood" Songs, Including Two by Ethan Hawke,
Enter Oscar Race,' *The Hollywood Reporter*, online, 7 November, www.
hollywoodreporter.com/race/three-boyhood-songs-including-two-746650 (accessed
20 June 2017).

Finley, L. (2014) *School Violence: A Reference Handbook*, 2nd ed., New York:
ABC-CLIO.

Fleming, M. (2014) 'What Was I Thinking? IFC President Jonathan Sehring on
Funding "Boyhood" for 12 Years,' *Deadline.com*, online, 14 September, http://
deadline.com/2014/09/boyhood-ifc-jonathan-sehring-funding-risk-834078/
(accessed 20 June 2017).

Gritten, D. (2015) '*Boyhood*: Richard Linklater Interview,' *The Telegraph*, online,
9 February, www.telegraph.co.uk/culture/film/starsandstories/10944351/Boyhood-
Richard-Linklater-interview.html (accessed 20 June 2017).

Grosz, C. (2014) '"Boyhood" Producer Cathleen Sutherland on How the Film's 12-Year Shoot Became "Rinse and Repeat",' *Deadline*, online, 11 December, http://deadline.com/2014/12/boyhood-producer-cathleen-sutherland-interview-12-year-production-1201320976/ (accessed 20 June 2017).

Harrod, M. (2010) 'The Aesthetics of Pastiche in the Work of Richard Linklater,' *Screen* 51:1, Spring, pp. 1–17.

Hawke, E. (2014) 'Ethan Hawke's Heartwarming Tribute to a "Boyhood" with Music,' *BuzzFeed*, online, 21 July, www.buzzfeed.com/ethanhawke/boyhood-the-black-album?utm_term=.ipGDlVWoz#.bw5n3wYZ9 (accessed 20 June 2017).

Hellman, M. (2004) 'On *It's Impossible to Learn to Plow by Reading Books*,' *Criterion*, online, 13 September, www.criterion.com/current/posts/1061-on-it-s-impossible-to-learn-to-plowby-reading-books (accessed 20 June 2017).

Hornaday, A. (2014) '"Boyhood" Movie Review: Richard Linklater's Audacious, Epic Cinematic Journey,' *The Washington Post*, online, 17 July, www.washingtonpost.com/goingoutguide/movies/boyhood-movie-review-richard-linklaters-audacious-epic-cinematic-journey/2014/07/17/99ef5f90-0064–11e4–8572–4b1b969b6322_story.html (accessed 20 June 2017).

Jagernauth, K. (2014) 'Harry Potter Gets the Richard Linklater Treatment in *Boyhood* Parody Trailer *Potterhood*,' *IndieWire*, online, 30 July, www.indiewire.com/2014/07/watch-harry-potter-gets-the-richard-linklater-treatment-in-boyhood-parody-trailer-potterhood-273977/ (accessed 20 June 2017).

Johnson, D. (2012) *Richard Linklater*, Urbana: University of Illinois Press.

Kachka, B. (2014) 'Ellar Coltrane Spent 12 Years Acting for Richard Linklater: Now What?,' *New York Magazine*, online, 30 June, www.vulture.com/2014/06/ellar-coltrane-on-his-12-year-movie-role.html (accessed 20 June 2017).

Kermode, M. (2014) '*Boyhood* Review – Richard Linklater Makes the Complex Appear Casual,' *The Guardian*, online, 13 July, www.theguardian.com/film/2014/jul/13/boyhood-richard-linklater-film-review (accessed 20 June 2017).

Kiang, J. (2014) 'Richard Linklater Discusses His 12-Year Project "Boyhood," Chronology, Memory & a Movie That Occurs Offscreen,' *IndieWire*, online, 18 February, www.indiewire.com/2014/02/richard-linklater-discusses-his-12-year-project-boyhood-chronology-memory-a-movie-that-occurs-offscreen-88939/ (accessed 20 June 2017).

Kierkegaard, S. (1843) *Papers and Journals*, selected and trans. A. Hannay [IV A 164], Hammondsworth, UK: Penguin, p. 161.

Kiuchi, Y. & Villarruel, F., eds. (2016) *The Young Are Making Their World: Essays on the Power of Youth Culture*, Jefferson, NC: McFarland.

Klein, A. (2011) *American Film Cycles: Reframing Genres, Screening Social Problems, and Defining Subcultures*, Austin: University of Texas Press.

Klinger, G. (n.d.) 'What Is *Boyhood*?,' *Cinema Scope*, online, http://cinema-scope.com/features/boyhood/ (accessed 20 June 2017).

Klosterman, C. (2005) 'Richard Linklater: The *Dazed and Confused* Director Explains Why Nostalgia is Mostly Bulls – t,' *Spin*, November, pp. 72–74.

Kohn, E. (2014) 'Richard Linklater Explains Why He Had to Make "Boyhood" and Keep It Under Wraps (Part 1),' *IndieWire*, online, 8 July, www.indiewire.

com/2014/07/richard-linklater-explains-why-he-had-to-make-boyhood-and-keep-it-under-wraps-part-1–24523/ (accessed 20 June 2017).

Labrecque, J. (2014a) 'Best of 2014: How Richard Linklater Cast His "Boyhood" Star,' *Entertainment Weekly*, online, 18 December, www.ew.com/article/2014/12/18/richard-linklater-boyhood-ellar-coltrane (accessed 20 June 2017).

Labrecque, J. (2014b) 'Patricia Arquette Is All-in for More "Boyhood",' *Entertainment Weekly*, online, 8 December, www.ew.com/article/2014/12/08/patricia-arquette-boyhood (accessed 20 June 2017).

Landau, J. (1997) 'Paul McCartney: Band on the Run,' *Rolling Stone*, online, 21 January, www.rollingstone.com/music/albumreviews/band-on-the-run-19970121 (accessed 20 June 2017).

Lang, B. (2015) 'Patricia Arquette's Comments Draw Praise, Unleash Controversy,' *Variety*, online, 23 February, http://variety.com/2015/film/news/patricia-arquette-comments-oscars-2015-controversy-1201439814/ (accessed 20 June 2017).

Lankes, M. (2014) *Boyhood: Twelve Years on Film*, Austin: University of Texas Press.

Lethem, J. (2016) 'The Moment Seizes You,' essay contained in liner notes to Criterion Collection (2016) *Boyhood* DVD.

Levy, E. (1999) *Cinema of Outsiders: The Rise of American Independent Film*, New York: New York University Press.

Lewis, H. (2014a) '"Boyhood": 11 Things to Know about Star Ellar Coltrane,' *The Hollywood Reporter*, online, 7 July, www.hollywoodreporter.com/news/meet-boyhood-kid-ellar-coltrane-718101 (accessed 20 June 2017).

Lewis, H. (2014b) 'Richard Linklater on "Boyhood's" Original Title, Casting Kid,' *The Hollywood Reporter*, online, 7 July, www.hollywoodreporter.com/news/richard-linklater-boyhoods-original-title-716894 (accessed 20 June 2017).

Lewis, J. (1992) *The Road to Romance and Ruin: Teen Films and Youth Culture*, New York: Routledge.

Linklater, R. (2014) 'Memories of the Present,' in Lankes, M., *Boyhood: Twelve Years on Film*, Austin: University of Texas Press, p. 8.

Linklater, R. (2017) Email correspondence with author, 12 March.

Livingston, G. (2015) 'Family Size among Mothers,' *Pew Research Center*, online, 7 May, www.pewsocialtrends.org/2015/05/07/family-size-among-mothers/ (accessed 20 June 2017).

Lowenstein, S., ed. (2009) *My First Movie: Take Two*, New York: Vintage.

Lucca, V. (2015) 'Interview: Sandra Adair,' *Film Comment*, online, 13 February, www.filmcomment.com/blog/interview-sandra-adair-boyhood/ (accessed 20 June 2017).

Matthews, J.D.H. (2016) 'AFI Awards,' *The Criterion Collection*, online, 11 December, www.criterion.com/lists/436854-afi-awards (accessed 20 June 2017).

McCarthy, T. (2014) '*Boyhood*: Sundance Review,' *The Hollywood Reporter*, online, 20 January, www.hollywoodreporter.com/review/boyhood-sundance-review-672531 (accessed 20 June 2017).

McKittrick, C. (2014) '"I Want to Tell a Story in a New Way": Linklater on *Boyhood*,' *Creative Screenwriting*, online, 29 December, https://creativescreenwriting.com/i-want-to-tell-a-story-in-a-new-way-linklater-on-boyhood/ (accessed 20 June 2017).

Mechanic, M. (2014) 'Meet the Star of "Boyhood," the Oscar Frontrunner Everybody's Talking About,' *Mother Jones*, online, 3 July, www.motherjones.com/media/2014/07/boyhood-movie-star-ellar-coltrane-interview (accessed 20 June 2017).

Mejia, P. (2014) 'Richard Linklater's "Boyhood" Projects a Spellbinding View of Memory,' *Newsweek*, online, 21 July, www.newsweek.com/richard-linklaters-boyhood-projects-spellbinding-view-memory-259995 (accessed 20 June 2017).

Merry, S. (2016) 'These Charts Show the Crazy Age Gap between Actors and Actresses Who Win Oscars,' *The Washington Post*, online, 29 February, www.washingtonpost.com/news/arts-and-entertainment/wp/2016/02/29/these-charts-show-the-huge-age-gap-between-actors-and-actresses-who-win-oscars/ (accessed 20 June 2017).

Meyer, C. (2014) 'A 12-Year Movie Shoot Became "Boyhood",' *The Sacramento Bee*, online, 28 July, www.sacbee.com/entertainment/movies-news-reviews/article2605143.html

Museum of Modern Art (2014) '*Boyhood*. 2014. Directed by Richard Linklater,' *MoMA*, online, www.moma.org/calendar/events/624?locale=en (accessed 20 June 2017).

Nash Information Services (2017) '*Boyhood* (2014),' *The Numbers*, online, www.the-numbers.com/movie/Boyhood (accessed 20 June 2017).

Nicholson, A. (2014) '*Eyes Wide Shut* at 15: Inside the Epic, Secretive Film Shoot That Pushed Tom Cruise and Nicole Kidman to Their Limits,' *Vanity Fair*, online, 17 July, www.vanityfair.com/hollywood/2014/07/eyes-wide-shut-tom-cruise-nicole-kidman (accessed 20 June 2017).

Nunez, M. (2015) 'A Trip Down Linklater Lane,' *The Huntsville Item*, online, 22 February, www.itemonline.com/news/a-trip-down-linklater-lane/article_5aff2af0-ba6c-11e4-aee1-af934aab87a7.html (accessed 20 June 2017).

O'Hehir, A. (2014) '*Boyhood*: Richard Linklater's 12-Year Family Masterpiece,' *Salon*, online, 10 July, www.salon.com/2014/07/10/boyhood_richard_linklaters_12_year_family_masterpiece/ (accessed 20 June 2017).

Paramount Home Entertainment (2014) *Boyhood* DVD, *Boyhood: 12 Years in the Making* featurette.

Peikert, M. (2014) 'Beth Sepko's Almost 12 Years Casting "Boyhood",' *Backstage*, online, 8 December, www.backstage.com/interview/beth-sepkos-almost-12-years-casting-boyhood/ (accessed 20 June 2017).

Pierson, J. (1995) *Spike, Mike, Slackers & Dykes: A Guided Tour across a Decade of American Independent Cinema*, New York: Hyperion and Miramax Books.

Pollock, C. (2017) 'Study: A Quarter of Texas Public Schools No Longer Teach Sex Ed,' *The Texas Tribune*, online, 14 February, www.texastribune.org/2017/02/14/texas-public-schools-largely-teach-abstinence-only-sex-education-repor/ (accessed 20 June 2017).

Puig, C. (2014) '"Boyhood": Portrait of a Child, Adolescent and Young Man,' *USA Today*, online, 10 July, www.usatoday.com/story/life/movies/2014/07/10/boyhood-movie-review/10636501/ (accessed 20 June 2017).

Rainer, P. (2014) '"Boyhood" Shows That Director Richard Linklater Is the Most Gifted Director of His Generation,' *Christian Science Monitor*, online, 11 July, www.csmonitor.com/The-Culture/Movies/2014/0711/Boyhood-shows-that-director-Richard-Linklater-is-the-most-gifted-director-of-his-generation (accessed 20 June 2017).

Rothman, L. (2014) 'Songs of the Time: Richard Linklater on the Music of *Boyhood*,' *Time*, online, 11 July, http://time.com/2964279/boyhood-music-richard-linklater-soundtrack/ (accessed 20 June 2017).

Schallenberg, G. (2016) 'Richard Linklater Bases Experiences as SHSU Baseball Player in New Film,' *The Huntsville Item*, online, 10 April, www.itemonline.com/sports/richard-linklater-bases-experiences-as-shsu-baseball-player-in-new/article_54366350-fed6-11e5-a6aa-53f4bfbce378.html (accessed 20 June 2017).

Schwartz, N. (2014) '"Boyhood": Richard Linklater's Divine Comedy,' *RogerEbert. com*, online, 7 August, www.rogerebert.com/balder-and-dash/boyhood-richard-linklaters-divine-comedy (accessed 20 June 2017).

Seymour, M. (2009) 'The Curious Case of Aging Visual Effects,' *fxguide*, online, 1 January, www.fxguide.com/featured/the_curious_case_of_aging_visual_effects/ (accessed 20 June 2017).

Shary, T. (1999) 'Reification and Loss in Postmodern Puberty: The Cultural Logic of Fredric Jameson and Young Adult Movies,' in Degli-Esposti, C. (ed.) *Postmodernism in the Cinema*, New York: Berghahn Books, pp. 73–89.

Shary, T. (2014) *Generation Multiplex: The Image of Youth in American Cinema since 1980*, Austin: University of Texas Press.

Shelton, R. (1982) 'Youth,' in *Selected Poems, 1969–1981*, Pittsburgh: University of Pittsburgh Press, p. 17.

Siegel, T. (2014) '"Boyhood": Why Richard Linklater Owns His New Movie,' *The Hollywood Reporter*, online, 19 June, www.hollywoodreporter.com/news/boyhood-why-richard-linklater-owns-712427 (accessed 20 June 2017).

Smith, C., Denton, M.L., Faris, R., & Regnerus, M. (2002) 'Mapping American Adolescent Religious Participation,' *Journal for the Scientific Study of Religion* 41:4, pp. 597–612.

Sperling, N. (2014) 'One Actor, One Kid, 12 Years, One Film: "Boyhood",' *Entertainment Weekly*, 17 July, pp. 31–32.

Steinmetz, K. (2014) 'Everything You Need to Know about the Making of *Boyhood* over 12 Years,' *Time*, online, 11 July, http://time.com/2974681/boyhood-movie-making-of-richard-linklater/ (accessed 20 June 2017).

Stevenson, S. (2014) 'This Little Space in Between,' *Slate*, online, 10 July, www.slate.com/articles/arts/culturebox/2014/07/boyhood_review_richard_linklater_movie_highlights_his_true_subject_as_a.html (accessed 20 June 2017).

Stone, R. (2013) *The Cinema of Richard Linklater: Walk, Don't Run*, New York: Wallflower and Columbia University Press.

Sundance Press Release (2014) '2014 Sundance Film Festival to Host Special Preview Screenings of *Boyhood* by Richard Linklater,' online, 13 January, www.sundance.org/blogs/news/2014-sundance-film-festival-will-preview-boyhood-from-richard-linklater (accessed 20 June 2017).

Taylor, T. (n.d.a) '*Boyhood* Was "Painful to Watch" for Lorelei Linklater,' *Dazed*, online, www.dazeddigital.com/artsandculture/article/20708/1/boyhood-was-painful-to-watch-for-lorelei-linklater (accessed 20 June 2017).

Taylor, T. (n.d.b) 'How Richard Linklater Soundtracked *Boyhood*,' *Dazed*, online, www.dazeddigital.com/music/article/22887/1/how-richard-linklater-soundtracked-boyhood (accessed 20 June 2017).

Thompson, K. (2015) 'Harry Potter and the Twelve-Year Boyhood,' *David Bordwell's Website on Cinema*, online, 15 March, www.davidbordwell.net/blog/2015/03/15/harry-potter-and-the-twelve-year-boyhood/ (accessed 20 June 2017).

Tobias, S. (2014) 'Richard Linklater Discusses the 12-Year Journey to *Boyhood*,' *The Dissolve*, online, 18 July, https://thedissolve.com/features/interview/666-interview-richard-linklater/ (accessed 20 June 2017).

Toronto Film Critics Association (2014) 'The Toronto Film Critics Association Names Richard Linklater's *Boyhood* the Best Film of the Year,' *TFCA*, online, 15 December, http://torontofilmcritics.com/features/and-the-winners-are/ (accessed 20 June 2017).

Travers, A. (2014) '"It's Everything and Nothing": Director Richard Linklater discusses "Boyhood",' *The Aspen Times*, online, 27 December, www.aspentimes.com/entertainment/activities-events/its-everything-and-nothing-director-richard-linklater-discusses-boyhood/ (accessed 20 June 2017).

Tropiano, S. (2006) *Rebels and Chicks: A History of the Hollywood Teen Movie*, New York: Back Stage Books.

Truffaut, F. (1957) 'You Are All Witnesses in This Trial: French Cinema Bursting Under Bogus Legends,' *Arts Magazine*, 15 May. Reprinted as 'Pleasing to the Eye,' *Cahiers du Cinéma*, 1987, pp. 223–224.

Vognar, C. (2014) 'Shot over 12 Years, "Boyhood" Is a Stirring Reminder to Cherish the Passages of Life,' *Dallas Morning News*, online, 17 July, www.dallasnews.com/arts/arts/2014/07/17/shot-over-12-years-boyhood-is-a-stirring-reminder-to-cherish-the-passages-of-life-a (accessed 20 June 2017).

Whipp, G. (2015) 'What "Boyhood" Cast, Director Learned about Family While Filming,' *Los Angeles Times*, online, 22 January, www.latimes.com/entertainment/envelope/la-et-mn-en-boyhood-column-20150122-column.html (accessed 20 June 2017).

Willis, H. (2014) 'It's about Time,' *Film Comment*, online, July/August, www.filmcomment.com/article/richard-linklater-boyhood/ (accessed 20 June 2017).

Woo, J. (2014) 'The One Scene in "Boyhood" No One Is Talking about,' *The Daily Dot*, online, 15 August, www.dailydot.com/via/one-scene-boyhood-no-one-talking/ (accessed 20 June 2017).

Zacharek, S. (2014) 'Linklater's Glorious *Boyhood* Captures Life in Bloom,' *The Village Voice*, online, 9 July, www.villagevoice.com/film/linklaters-glorious-boyhood-captures-life-in-bloom-6442349 (accessed 20 June 2017).

Index

Page numbers in italic refer to a figure on the corresponding page.

Rowling, J.K. 7
Ruiz, Roland 83
'Ryan's Song' (song) 68

Salmon, Bruce 89n11
same-sex marriage 27
Sam Houston State University 16, 24n2
Samsara (2011) 8
San Antonio, Texas 60
San Marcos, Texas 60
Saved! (2004) 12
schooling 3–4, 6, 9, 15n9, 20, 27–8, 30,
   40, 83, 99, 102–3
School of Rock (2003) 2, 11, 22, 52n13
schools: elementary 16, 35, 51; high 16,
   61, 63, 65, 70–1, 78–9, 100; middle
   51, 59, 61, 101
Scream (1996) 12
Screen Actors Guild 93
script *see Boyhood*: script
Sehring, Jonathan 22, 92
Sepko, Beth 18
Seven Up! (1964) 8
sexism 56, 71; *see also* homophobia
Sexton, Charlie 44
sexual activity 4, 10–12, 32, 56–7,
   62–3, 88n1; *see also* kissing;
   pregnancy; virginity
sexuality 11–13, 27, 54, 60, 62, 97;
   see also gender; homoeroticism;
   young sexuality
Shaw, Indica 89n11
sibling rivalry 31–2, 34, 45, 51
siblings 31–2, 34, 45, 49–51; *see also*
   stepsiblings
Siegel, Tatiana 22
Simmons, J.K. 94
Singles (1992) 11
Sixteen Candles (1984) 11
skateboarding 48
Slacker (1991) 1, *2*, 11, 17, 21, 24, 60,
   77
slasher films 11
Sloss, John 22
smartphones 13, 27, 35, 74–5, *76*
Smith, Elijah 30
Smokes and Lollies (1976) 14n8
smoking 52n12, 65, 89n18
social media 35, 56, 75, 92; *see also*
   Facebook; internet; YouTube

society 8, 13, 26, 96–7, 102–3; *see also*
   consumer culture; demographics;
   popular culture
soundtrack *see Boyhood*: music
Sperling, Nicole 18
sports 28, 44, 98; *see also* baseball;
   bowling; football; skateboarding;
   swimming
Standing Up (2013) 4
Star Wars (1977) 11, 58
stepchildren 41, 66
stepsiblings 39, *41*, 49; *see also*
   siblings
Stolen Kisses (1968) 14n3
Straight Out of Brooklyn (1991) 11
SubUrbia (1996) 2, 11
suicide 60
Sul Ross State University 85
Sundance Film Festival 3, 23–4, 91
Superman (1978) 11
Sutherland, Cathleen 22–3, 89
swimming 57
symbolism *see Boyhood*: symbolism

Tamagotchi 53n15
Tape (2001) 12, 17–18, 53n14
teachers 16, 19, 30, 35, 39, 47,
   51, 70–1, 78, 99, 101; *see also*
   schooling; schools
technology 7, 13, 21, 23, 35, 49, 52–3,
   74–6, 84; *see also* computers; internet;
   social media; video; video games
Teenage Rebel (1956) 10
teenagers 4, 6, 9, 11–12, 56, 70, 75,
   78, 102–3; *see also* adolescence;
   childhood; youth
teen movies 4, 6, 10–13, 54, 68, 97,
   101
television 10, 31, 37, 47, 52
Temple, Shirley 4, 9
terrorism 26, 96
Texas 5, 16, 35–6, 53n19, 55, 67–8, 85,
   88n1, 102; *see also specific places
   in*; University of
Texas Pledge 36, 53n19
Texas State University 60, 83
theatrical release *see Boyhood*:
   theatrical release
Thief and the Cobbler, The (1995) 8
Thompson, Evie 60

For further information and instructions, please contact our
distributor: GPSR@mare-nostrum.co.uk Easton Business Centre,
Station Approach, TQ13 7PD Newton Abbot, Germany

For Product Safety Concerns and Information please contact our
EU representative GPSR@taylorandfrancis.com Taylor & Francis
Verlag GmbH, Kaufingerstraße 24, 80331 München, Germany